Twayne's English Authors Series

EDITOR OF THIS VOLUME

Arthur Kinney

University of Massachusetts

Richard Crashaw

A HYMN

to the name · and honour of
the renowned

S. TERESIA

Foundres of the Reformation of the Order of
barefoote Carmelites ;

A Woman

for Angelicall *height* of Contemplation ,
for Masculine *courage* of Performance ,
more then a woman .

Who yet a Child
outranne Maturity ,
& durst plott a Martyrdome ;
but was reserved by God
to dy the liuing death of the life of his loue .
of whose great impressions
as her noble heart had most high experiment,
so hath she in her life most heroically exprest them ,
in her Spirituall posterity most fruitfully propagated them ,
and in these her heaunly writings
most sublimely , most sweetly
taught them to ÿ world .

:

Love, thou art absolute. sole Lord
Of life & death. To prove the word
Wee'l need to goe to none of ÿ all

Thos:

RICHARD CRASHAW

By PAUL A. PARRISH
Texas A&M University

TWAYNE PUBLISHERS
A DIVISION OF G. K. HALL & CO., BOSTON

Frontispiece photo of the title page of Richard Crashaw's poem:
"A Hymn to the Name and Honour of the Renowned S. Teresia . . ."
appears courtesy of The Pierpont Morgan Library

Library of Congress Cataloging in Publication Data

Parrish, Paul A.   1944–
Richard Crashaw.

(Twayne's English authors series; TEAS 299)
Bibliography: p. 182–85
Includes index.
1. Crashaw, Richard, 1613?–1649—Criticism and
interpretation.
PR3386.P3   1980   821'.4   80–14468
ISBN 0-8057-6791-6

For Linda, Marc, and Gavin

Contents

About the Author

Paul A. Parrish received his B.A. in English from Abilene Christian University (then Abilene Christian College) in 1966. He went on to the University of Kansas, where he received his M.A. in English two years later. Professor Parrish received his Ph.D. in 1971 from Rice University. His doctoral studies concentrated on English literature of the Renaissance and seventeenth century, and he completed a dissertation on John Donne's two *Anniversary* Poems. Professor Parrish is now an Associate Professor of English at Texas A&M University. His publications include articles on Elizabeth Bowen (in *Critique*), Ralph Ellison (in *Renascence*), and articles or reviews on Renaissance studies in *Studies in Short Fiction, Criticism, Papers on Language and Literature,* and *Concerning Poetry.* In 1977 Winthrop Publishers brought out his anthology of literature entitled *Celebration: Introduction to Literature.*

Preface

Fundamentally, this study of Richard Crashaw serves as an introduction to his life and his works. The essential scheme of the book is easily drawn: the first long chapter discusses the pattern of his life and art, and in it I attempt to suggest related developments in his personal history and his poetry as we progress from the late 1620s to the late 1640s. Having presented these historical and artistic contexts, I proceed to discuss the poems, following a synthesis of generic and chronological divisions within his works.

I believe that there is a need for a new and thorough study of Crashaw, and in saying that I do not mean to appear unapprecia-tive of past criticism and scholarship. On the contrary, my indebtedness to the work of others is extensive and will be quite apparent to readers familiar with studies of Crashaw. The work of Austin Warren, Ruth Wallerstein, and Mario Praz is especially formidable, and, while I have made specific acknowledgments in comments and notes, I recognize an indebtedness that is more encompassing than such particular citations allow. Nonetheless, there is value, I believe, in a reconsideration of the whole of Crashaw's life and art, leading to a study that reflects more recent criticism and scholarship and that suggests a less idiosyncratic role for Crashaw in the history of English poetry. My book does nothing to undermine the ultimate stature of Crashaw as a Baroque poet; indeed, it is from that dominant perception that I interpret his major poems in the last several chapters. But I also encourage a recognition of greater variety in Crashaw's poetic achievement and discourage a temptation to reduce his art—as any critical label will result in reduction—to the "Baroque." I hope that the book is judged to respond to Crashaw with a relatively fresh and open approach, not neglecting the weight of past judgments but not assuming them to be necessarily or thoroughly true.

Portions of two chapters have appeared previously in print. My remarks on "The Weeper" in Chapter 4 are adapted from my article "Crashaw's Two Weepers" in *Concerning Poetry* 10:2 (1977): 47–59; comments on Crashaw's funeral elegies in Chapter 3 are drawn from my longer essay appearing as part of Robert M. Cooper's collection of critical essays. I am grateful to *Concerning Poetry* and to Professor Cooper for permission to reprint this material. Students of Crashaw are fortunate in having two first-rate modern editions of his complete poetry: L. C. Martin's *The Poems English, Latin, and Greek of Richard Crashaw*, published in the Oxford English Texts Series, and George W. Williams's *The Complete Poetry of Richard Crashaw*, originally published in the Anchor Seventeenth-Century Series. Professor Williams's edition, from which I have established the texts of Crashaw's poetry, is particularly accessible in that it prints differing versions of a poem on facing pages, it includes the originals of Crashaw's translations, and it provides English translations of Crashaw's Latin poems. For permission to quote from *The Complete Poetry of Richard Crashaw* I thank Doubleday & Company, Inc. For quotations from other sources I have retained original spelling; I have, however, followed the commonly accepted practice of modernizing a few specific letters and words— i, j, u, v, y^e (for *the*), and y^t (for *that*).

I have been assisted in the completion of this study by numerous individuals and institutions. I received generous grants from two sources at Texas A&M University, the College of Liberal Arts and the Research Foundation. I was further provided with a grant from the Penrose Fund of the American Philosophical Society that enabled me to do important work in England during the final summer of this project. Libraries and library personnel have been responsive to my requests and accommodating in granting me access to materials. Specifically, I wish to thank the library staffs at Texas A&M, the Humanities Research Center at the University of Texas at Austin, and the Bancroft Library at the University of California at Berkeley. In England, the staffs of the British Library, the Bodleian Library, Oxford, and the Cambridge University Library provided valuable assistance and ready access to rare holdings. Mr. Hilton Kelliher of the Department of Manuscripts of the British Library allowed me to examine materials in his possession and shared with me his insights on Crashaw's life and art.

Several colleagues at Texas A&M were generous with time and

counsel. Stanley Archer and Norman Grabo read earlier versions of portions of two chapters, and David Stewart offered continuing support as department chairman. Anthony O'Keeffe, Katherine O'Keeffe, and Larry Reynolds provided personal and professional encouragement and made important suggestions for improving the manuscript. I thank them for their friendship and for their help in making the book better than it would otherwise have been. I also thank Arthur Kinney of the University of Massachusetts, Amherst, who read the completed manuscript and who was encouraging about its publication. My wife, Linda, and my children, Marc and Gavin, accepted, with kindness and calm, the emotional peaks and valleys that come with a project of this duration. Linda, herself a university professor, no doubt understood the particular reasons for the occasional strain on time, energy, and patience. Marc and Gavin, whose age prevented that kind of understanding, had to wonder more simply, but to them no less significantly, about the times I was working on "the book" and was thus unable to do more important things, like playing soccer, reading books, or watching "Sesame Street." At times I think that my determination to complete this project was due in no small part to my desire to dedicate it to those who mean the most to me.

PAUL A. PARRISH

Texas A&M University

Chronology

CHAPTER 1

Backgrounds: The Life and the Art

I The Historical Setting

THE English church of the first half of the seventeenth century found its historically claimed position as a balanced and ideal *via media* difficult to assert and maintain. Challenged from without by the Roman church and assailed from within by dissenters, schismatics, and Puritans, the Church of England was marked by recurring conflict and controversy for all of the forty years of the century preceding the ascendancy of Puritanism and the Commonwealth. The conflict between Anglican and Catholic is in some ways more easily drawn because it involved two distinct religious and national bodies formally separated and formally committed to different liturgical forms, different doctrines, different conceptions of the priesthood, and, most obviously, radically different views of the supremacy of the Pope. Alike though Anglican and Roman may appear to have been from our modern perspective, the gulf between seventeenth-century Canterbury and Rome was certain and fixed. Controversy within the Anglican communion, at times more torturous and threatening than that from without, is also more difficult to untangle and define.

Controversies between Puritan and High Churchman, though often bitter and irreconcilable, initially involve warring factions that remain members of the same communion. Puritanism during this period is thus "a body of dissident opinion *within* the established Church, held by men who wanted to jettison the freight of tradition, men more rigidly scripturalists and in terror of Catholic elements."[1] The abiding concern of the Puritan mind was that the English church was only partially reformed and that in such a state its practices and beliefs frequently reflected a Roman influence. These spiritual residents of Geneva attacked, therefore, Anglican doctrines and liturgy that placed Canterbury, in their eyes, too near to Rome.

Among the dominant issues in the ongoing controversy between Puritan and High Churchman were the Puritan concerns with reformed purity, inward sanctity, and the requisite priority of faith. To the High Church plea for a recognition of tradition in church matters, the Puritan answered with a call for closer attention to scripture and for a reformation of a tradition that was in danger of corruption. A High Churchman followed the direction of Archbishop Laud (1573–1645) in a revival of church liturgy and in the primacy of love and good works; the Puritan urged added simplicity in worship, the efficacy of personal sanctity, and the primacy of faith. The Puritan feared the excesses of elaborate clerical garb and expensive ornaments and artifacts within and without the church building. Laud and his followers encouraged more uniform and distinct clerical dress and expensively outfitted church houses as an outward sign of the unique value of Christ. Puritans elevated preaching and chose to give greater prominence to the pulpit in the church house; the High Churchman elevated prayer and the sacraments and argued with equal vehemence for the necessary elevation of the altar, both symbolically and physically. So strong was the Puritan emphasis on preaching that permanent lectureships were established among Puritan supporters, and Puritan lecturers traveled throughout England, only to meet head on the opposition of Laud.[2]

In spite of the increasing vehemence with which Puritan and High Anglican dealt with each other, however, not until the fifth decade of the century was the separation irrevocable. Indeed one point on which there was general agreement between these two otherwise conflicting forces was the danger posed by Roman influence. If Puritans conceived that Laud was tending toward Catholic doctrine and belief, that conception was not shared by most orthodox Anglicans. During his trial and just before his execution, Laud vigorously denied the charges of "popery" and professed himself a loyal member of the "protestant church of England."[3] One of Laud's principal supporters, John Cosin, Master of Peterhouse and Vice-Chancellor of Cambridge at a time when the university was being accused of encouraging Roman practices, promptly disinherited a son who converted formally to Rome.[4] The feud between Puritan and Anglican was thus, at least at the beginning of the century, a fight between two brothers, though as we move through the first four decades we realize, as well, that the Puritan came increasingly to see the Anglican as, if a brother at all, at least a very soiled and disreputable one. Adding to the hostilities were the political alliances that colored the positions of both groups, so that Puritan and Parliament opposed Laudian and Royalist to a point where eventually the schism widened to unbridgeable proportions. Still, the most open conflict during the early part of the century was that between the Roman and English churches, for we see in that conflict a war between two distinct ideological and religious families.

The analogy to a war between Roman and English factions is at times painfully appropriate, as the potentiality for threats, executions, and murders was never far from the surface of English life. The most dramatic evidence of this fact was the Gunpowder Plot of 1605. On November 5 of that year Guy Fawkes and several Roman Catholic conspirators were arrested and charged with planning to blow up the House of Parliament when King James and his two sons were in attendance. That event proved to be a *cause célèbre* that further accelerated the already significant antagonism felt by Catholics and Anglicans alike. In spite of this and other physical manifestations, however, the religious-political war was not fought in the streets or on the battlefield as much as on the printed page. In that war William Crashaw, preacher, scholar, and occasional poet, was a frequent combatant.

Born at Handsworth in 1572 and educated at St. John's College, Cambridge, William Crashaw held numerous preaching assignments before his death in 1626.[5] Among his pastorates were those at Inner Temple, London, and, from 1618 until his death, St. Mary Matfellon, Whitechapel, London. About his preaching or other circumstances of his pastoral life we know very little; about his theology, as evidenced in his writings, we can know a good deal.

William Crashaw was an avowed opponent of all things smacking of a Roman influence, and he wrote numerous polemical treatises denouncing the religion he portrays in his will as "the heape and chaos of all heresies and the channell whereinto the fowlest impieties & heresies that have byne in the christian Worlde have runn and closelye emptied themselves."[6] The Roman church was, for him, a "Babylon that will not bee healed," and in the *Jesuites Gospell* (1610) he advances further the frequent Protestant claim that the Pope was the Antichrist, a view reiterated in his will:

"I beleeve the Popes seate and power to be the power of the greate Antichrist and the doctrine of the Pope (as nowe it is) to be the doctrine of Antechriste yea that doctrine of devills prophecied of by the Apostle And that the true and absolute Papist soe livinge and dyeinge debarres himself of salvation for oughte that we knowe."[7]

William Crashaw was both forthright and prolific in his denunciation of Catholicism, most especially of all things related to the Jesuits.[8] In spite of his sometimes hysterical fear of the dangers of Roman activity, however, William Crashaw was not one to shun the writings of those he denounced. On the contrary, he amassed an impressive library of writings by and about Catholics and ended up with what has been called "one of the finest private theological libraries of the time."[9] In 1614, while communicating with St. John's College to secure their interest in purchasing his library, Crashaw referred to his collection as amounting to some 3,000 books and 500 manuscripts.[10]

The life and writings of William Crashaw appear to have had one common purpose: to affirm the one true faith as he saw it and to frustrate the threat that to him was most ominous and powerful—Roman Catholicism. In his opposition to Rome, Crashaw has, of course, many companions, but we cannot be certain, as earlier commentators assumed, that William Crashaw's strong antipapist stance places him in the Puritan camp. Other orthodox Anglicans, including Laud and Cosin, vigorously opposed papal influence on English life, for however much Anglican writers and theologians felt threatened on the one side by Puritans, few dared to avow sympathy or support for doctrines and practices that might be judged of Roman origin.[11] Nonetheless, what remains pronounced and distinct in William Crashaw's writings is the unqualified vehemence of his antipapist statements. Others were concerned about the possibility of a growing Roman influence; William Crashaw seems to have been obsessed. Less than ten years after his death, the simplistic antipapist dogma evident in the writings of William Crashaw and others is satirized and attacked:

> O he is Antichrist:
> Doubt this, and doubt (say they) that Christ is Christ.
> Why, 'tis a point of Faith. What e're it be,
> I'm sure it is no point of Charitie.
> In summe, no longer shall our people hope,
> To be a true Protestant, 's but to hate the Pope.

The writer of these verses was William Crashaw's one child, Richard, who was later to become one of the most famous converts to Catholicism of his day, a living witness to the faith his father spent half a lifetime denouncing.

A. Richard Crashaw's Early Years

The dramatic contrast between his father's numerous writings and Richard Crashaw's eventual conversion, though accurate and important, is also misleading. For there is little doubt that Richard Crashaw moved steadily, not suddenly, toward his eventual allegiance to Rome. Four environs dominated Richard Crashaw's life until the mid-1640s, and it is likely that each succeeding locale and its citizenry influenced him toward the High Anglicanism he espoused before his conversion. From his home life with his father, to Charterhouse school in London, to Pembroke College, Cambridge, and finally to Peterhouse, Cambridge, Crashaw witnessed increasing support of the Laudian movement and its elevation of the liturgy, church luxury, and love. By the time he left Peterhouse, under forced exile, he was prepared for the next step in his progress, though a dramatic and perhaps painful step it must have been—conversion to Rome.

Richard Crashaw was born in 1612 or 1613 to William Crashaw and his first wife. Some time before 1619 Richard's mother died, for it was in that year that his father was married a second time, to Elizabeth Skinner. Of the family life provided for young Richard we know little, but there is some evidence of affection and attention from both mother and father. Elizabeth Crashaw died in childbirth in 1620 and shortly thereafter appeared a commemorative volume, *The Honour of Vertue or The Monument erected by the sorowfull Husband . . .*, and in that tribute we are told of Elizabeth's "singular motherly affection to the child of her predecessor."[12] When William Crashaw died six years after his second wife, in 1626, Richard was named coexecutor of the will, although no special provisions for him are indicated. An early biographer, David Lloyd, records that young Richard showed so much promise as a scholar that he was, following the death of his father, taken under the care of two lawyers, Sir Henry Yelverton and Sir Randolph Crew, "the one paying for his *Diet*, the other for his *Cloaths*, Books, and Schooling till he was provided of both in the Royal Foundation at *Charterhouse*."[13]

No records exist to confirm Richard Crashaw's earliest schooling, but he was apparently admitted to Charterhouse School in 1629. The Charterhouse Free School and Hospital had been founded in 1611 by Thomas Sutton, who made provisions in his will to provide continuing care for elderly men (in the "Brotherhood" of the Hospital) and young school-age boys (through the "School Foundation"). Sutton's will provided for the admission of forty Foundation Scholars ("Gownboys") who would receive sustenance and a sound classical education from the Charterhouse masters and who would adhere to the rigorous discipline of life at the school. A gownboy such as Crashaw "rose at 5 a.m., he had his breakfast at 8 a.m.—beer, bread, and cheese. His dinner seems to have been at 3 p.m. . . . with a supper of bread and cheese and beer at night. . . . Gownboys had to sleep two in a bed till the year 1805."[14] Between meals time was devoted to reading, writing, and studying in classical disciplines. The prestige of Charterhouse is confirmed by the list of governors of the school. Among the first governors in 1611 were George Abbott, Archbishop of Canterbury; Lancelot Andrewes, Bishop of Ely; and Sir Edward Coke, Lord Chief Justice of England. Later governors include Francis Beaumont (1617), John Donne (1626), and William Laud (1628). Also appointed governor in 1628 was Randolph Crew, Crashaw's guardian, and it is likely that through his influence Crashaw was admitted to the school.

Lloyd emphasizes the value of Crashaw's Charterhouse years in developing his poetic talents and in providing the significant influence of the Master of Charterhouse, Robert Brooke. Of Crashaw, Lloyd writes:

his nature being leisurely advanced by Art, and his own pretty conceits improved by those of the choicest Orators and Poets, which he was not onely taught to understand, but imitate and make, not only their rich sense his own, but to smooth his soul as well as fill it . . . ; the essays Mr. *Brooks* [sic] . . . imposed upon him, on the Epistles and Gospels, at School, were the ground of that Divine fancy, so famous in *Pembroke-hall*, where he was Scholar; and *Peter-house*, where he was Fellow, in Cambridge.[15]

The "essays" here referred to are probably sacred epigrams, some of which Crashaw may later have collected and published in his 1634 *Epigrammatum Sacrorum Liber*. Additional evidence both for the early dating of some of the epigrams and for the decisive influence of Brooke is seen in the prefatory poem on Brooke that accompanies the 1634 volume. Crashaw praises Brooke as a Master who was not quick to use the rod but who established instead a mild authority ("mitia jura"). In ultimate tribute Crashaw puns on his Master's name, portraying him, not as a "brook" but as an important spring ("non parvi . . . fontis") that yields the offspring ("soboles") of this book.[16]

Beyond his influence as Master and educator, Brooke may also have contributed to the development of Crashaw's political and religious views. Some twelve years after Crashaw's departure to Cambridge, Brooke was expelled as Master of Charterhouse by Parliament. According to Gerald Davies, historian of Charterhouse, the action was "a sequel to a resolution by a Committee of the House of Commons, who had sequestered him for 'certen misdemeanors.' Brooke's misdemeanour was his avowed adherence to the Royalist cause, and his having impressed his views upon his pupils, two of whom were the poets Richard Crashaw and Richard Lovelace."[17] While the extent of Brooke's influence remains in doubt, it is surely more than coincidence that Brooke, who must have been the first lasting influence on Crashaw after his father died, would fall victim to the same Parliamentary sword that was wielded against his former pupil at Cambridge.

Crashaw was already writing poetry of some note during his Charterhouse years and attention was being paid. In addition to some Latin epigrams, the poems on the Gunpowder Treason and the king's coronation, as well as other Latin verses and the translation of Psalm 23, probably come from this period.[18] The Gunpowder Treason poems confirm that, to this point, Crashaw is still very much his father's son. The Catholic plotters are associated with the night and darkness; they are "the monster" that Heaven must kick down to Pluto's porch. Further evidence of Crashaw's embryonic but growing reputation as a poet is seen in the fact that, while still fresh on the Cambridge scene, Crashaw contributed to several commemorative volumes compiled by the university and, as early as 1631, presented the poem that appears under the portrait of Lancelot Andrewes in a volume of Andrewes's collected sermons.

B. Pembroke College

For schoolboys leaving Charterhouse one of two alternatives was proposed. Some were apprenticed in the trades; others of greater intellectual capability were encouraged to pursue further education at the university. "The boy who was by acquirements and promise fit for the University, and for the professions to which it was an entrance, was to be sent there with an exhibition" (a grant from the sponsoring school).[19] Crashaw was judged "fit for the University," and he was, accordingly, admitted to Pembroke College on July 6, 1631.

On October 2, 1631, Crashaw was elected to a Greek Scholarship under the provisions of the Watt Foundation. Candidates for these awards were to be "of good hope and towardness for witt and memory, like to continue the course of learning, and well affected toward religion, and the ministery Ecclesiasticall." Furthermore, they were, at the time of appointment, to demonstrate skill in Latin, Greek, and Hebrew and to be capable of translating a book of the *Iliad* and Hebrew psalms.[20] In return for support from the Foundation, a Greek Scholar had specific oratorical and poetic duties. As one requirement, each Scholar was to "make verses. 4 Hexam. Pentam. Latin as many Greeks of the same matter at Circumcision, Epiphany, Purification, Annunciation, Easter, Ascension, Pentecost, Trinity Sun, All Sts, Xtmas, Good friday. 2 greeke 2 Latin e'ry Sunday other holy day."[21] The poetic discipline of writing sacred epigrams, promoted by Brooke at Charterhouse, was thus continued at Pembroke. It is no surprise, therefore, that the first volume of poetry put forward exclusively in Crashaw's name was his volume of sacred epigrams.

Crashaw's contemporary reputation as a poet, undoubtedly enhanced by the publication of *Epigrammatum Sacrorum Liber*, was at least modestly secure even without that volume. Anthony à Wood comments (in *Athenae Oxonienses*, 1691) that Crashaw's reputation, confirmed at Peterhouse, was evident earlier at Pembroke; at both colleges "his admirable faculty in Latin and English Poetry was well known."[22] Most of Crashaw's secular verse comes from this period, and numerous elegiac pieces on Cambridge contemporaries or laudatory pieces on the royal family can be dated with relative accuracy. Both the publication of his separate volume of epigrams and his frequent appearance in Cambridge collections substantiate his early esteem as a poet.

Warren and others have demonstrated convincingly that the development of Crashaw's High Anglican sentiments, and eventually his conversion to Catholicism, find their principal impetus in his associations at Peterhouse. It is also true that Pembroke nurtured the same temperament. The High Anglican viewpoint had been dominant at Pembroke since Lancelot Andrewes was Master, and that spirit continued during Crashaw's years under the Mastership of Benjamin Laney.[23] In his epistles dedicatory to Laney (for a manuscript collection of epigrams and for *Epigrammatum Sacrorum Liber*) Crashaw praises his master for his efforts to beautify and embellish the college chapel and thus make religion more elegant—an action, as we have seen, anathema to a Puritan but sacred to a High Churchman. Under Laney religion is allowed to appear in a more pleasant form ("amæniori facie"), adorned as a most beautiful goddess ("pulcherrima dea"). The holy house of God is restored to an appropriate luster ("nitorem") that in turn reflects favorably on Laney himself.[24] In the poem that follows the prose preface to the volume of epigrams, Laney is commended further for his efforts to adorn religion, and the dedicatory pieces together thus ring as a tribute to Laney's Laudian sensibilities.

Laney was not the only member of Pembroke openly to challenge the Puritans and defend the High Anglican position. The Rev. John Tourney, Crashaw's tutor at Pembroke, was twice called before the Vice-Chancellor of the University during a brief period in 1634 for preaching sermons questioning the Doctrine of Justification by Faith only—of singular significance to the Puritans. Tourney was released unpunished, to the disappointment of a Puritan observer who complains of the "great Abettors of Mr. Tourney" and of the increasing tolerance of "Novelties, both in Rites and Doctrines." The same writer, Dr. Ward, Master of Sidney College, also notes that those who favor Puritans are increasingly "disgraced and checked" in their efforts.[25] Crashaw's attitude toward Tourney and his view of the controversy fomented by Tourney's sermons and the Doctrine of Justification by Faith are indicated in two poems. The first is found in the preliminary material of the *Epigrammatum*, along with the tributes to Laney and Brooke. There Tourney is praised as Crashaw's most honored tutor ("Tutori suo summè observando"), who is in part responsible for the poetic "child"—the volume of poems—there revealed. The second poem, which quite likely results from the specific controversy over Tourney's sermons, is Crashaw's Latin work titled "Fides quæ sola justificat, non est sine Spe & Dilectione" (Faith which alone justifies, does not exist without hope and love). Crashaw does not argue against the eleventh of the Thirty-Nine

Articles, but he does urge a focus more compatible with the High
Anglican, rather than the Puritan, position: "Nam neque tam *sola*
est" (For it does not exist so *alone*). The aim to balance faith and
love is crucial, arising as it does out of a context where faith is the
more Protestant, and certainly the more Puritan, emphasis. Without love, Crashaw says, faith is already dead ("Mortua jam nunc
est"), and he concludes the poem with a plea not to have faith that
exists in isolation: "Quæ sibi tam nimia est, sit mihi nulla Fides"
(Let there be for me no Faith which is much too much to itself).

   Another controversial occasion provides yet a further example
of Crashaw's religious attitude during these years. In 1635, Robert
Shelford published a work titled *Five Pious and Learned Dis-
courses*, in which he presented sermons on various doctrines and
practices. His views support the High Anglican position on such
matters as the hierarchical position of love, the insufficiency of
faith alone, the virtue of embellishing God's house. Archbishop
Ussher, writing to Dr. Ward from Drogheda, Ireland, expresses
great alarm at the aid "such rotten stuff as Shelford hath vented"
provides for the Roman cause: "The Jesuits of England sent over
the book hither to confirm our papists in their obstinacy, and to
assure them that we are now coming home unto them as fast as we
can."[26] Crashaw's response to the Shelford text is unequivocal. His
poem "Upon the ensuing Treatises" (later, "On a Treatise of
Charity") was published in Shelford's 1635 volume and exhibits
effusive praise for some of the very ideas most objectionable to the
Puritans, notably the value of a fulsome liturgy in worship and the
elevation of love over faith. "Gods services," he says, "no longer
shall put on/A *sluttishnesse*, for *pure religion*." Worship will not be
characterized by "dead Devotion" nor will it "keep/A melancholy
mansion in those cold/Urns." Without slighting faith, Crashaw,
like Shelford, establishes the priority of love. Too often, the poet
indicates, we "swell *a name*/Of faith, *a mountaine word*, made up
of aire" and in the process turn charity "out to tremble in the cold."
Finally, while clearly espousing no Roman point of view, Crashaw
exposes the inadequacy of faith that rests largely on an antipapist
stance. He particularly ridicules the extreme Protestant claim that
the Pope is the Antichrist, concluding with the lines cited earlier:
"In summe, no longer shall our people hope,/To be a true
Protestant, 's but to hate the Pope."

C. Little Gidding and Peterhouse, Cambridge

A year before the publication of the Shelford volume Crashaw graduated B.A. from Pembroke. Shortly thereafter, some time in 1635, he was elected to a Fellowship at Peterhouse, where he proceeded M.A. in 1638 and where he spent the remainder of his Cambridge years. At Peterhouse Crashaw found a religious atmosphere extraordinarily compatible with his own temperament. For a young man moving further away from the severe faith of his father and gradually toward the warmth and luxury of Rome, Peterhouse provided emotional nourishment within the security of Anglican orthodoxy.

Contemporary documents do not reveal many details about Crashaw's life at Peterhouse, but we may assume that it was very satisfying for him. His duties at Peterhouse were not rigorous; he apparently had only three students under his tutorship while he was there.[27] He was ordained sometime during the years 1635–1639, although there are no surviving records to provide an exact dating. The *terminus ad quem* is 1639, by which time he was curate of Little St. Mary's, the church historically and emotionally tied to the college at Peterhouse. More exactly, Crashaw was both catechist at Peterhouse and curate of Little St. Mary's. As curate he was an assistant to the resident minister of the parish; as catechist, he was a "theological tutor or lecturer."[28]

The author of the Preface to the 1646 and 1648 editions of *Steps to the Temple*, presumably an unnamed acquaintance at Cambridge, comments on Crashaw's attachment to Little St. Mary's and on the spiritual nourishment the church provided:

Reader, we stile his Sacred Poems, *Stepps to the Temple*, and aptly, for in the Temple of God, under his wing, he led his life in St. *Maries* Church neere St. *Peters* Colledge: There he lodged under *Tertullian's* roofe of Angels: There he made his nest more gladly then *David's* Swallow neere the house of God: where like a primitive Saint, he offered more prayers in the night, then others usually offer in the day; There he penned these Poems, *Stepps* for happy soules to climbe heaven by.[29]

Both this writer and Lloyd comment on Crashaw's academic achievements, notably his skill in languages, and Lloyd makes a

particular point of emphasizing his oratorical skill as a preacher: his
"thronged Sermons . . . ravished more like Poems . . . scattering
not so much Sentences . . . [as] Extasies, his soul brea[t]hing in
each word, was the soul of the Assembly, as its original is of the
World."[30]

Crashaw's years at Peterhouse (1635–1643) were undoubtedly
the most fulfilling of his life. Had he been able to stay in such
surroundings he would probably have died in the communion of
the Anglican church. Two influences must have been most
dominant on the young preacher and poet. One was the religious
community at Little Gidding; the other, more pervasive, was the
weighty High Anglican and Royalist viewpoint that governed the
entire college of Peterhouse during the years of Crashaw's
residency.

The community of Little Gidding had been established in 1626
by Nicholas Ferrar and his mother as a religious retreat and as an
alternative to the public life that each, especially Nicholas, had
experienced. In 1624, the same year Nicholas Ferrar's public
service culminated in his election to Parliament, his mother
purchased Little Gidding in Huntingdonshire. At the time the
property looked quite unlike a devotional setting: it consisted of a
shepherd's hut, a decaying manor house, and a church—used at the
time as a barn. But for the Ferrars, who had earlier rejected two
other sites as being too public, it had the one most required
element: privacy. The Ferrars set about to create the setting in
which each could follow Nicholas's dictum: "to devote myself to
God, and to go into a religious retirement."[31]

Life at Little Gidding was exacting and controlled: daily offices
were observed, one for each hour, meals were silent, and there was
a continual observance of prayer and praise throughout the day
and night. Crashaw's "Description of a Religious House," probably
inspired in part by Little Gidding, captures the rigor and routine of
the disciplined life, the "hasty Portion of praescribed sleep," the
hands "full of harty labours," the constant effort that is "work for
work, not wages." But the poem also confirms the peace and
satisfaction that such a life brings to willing participants:

> reverent discipline, and religious fear,
> And soft obedience, find sweet biding here;
> Silence, and sacred rest; peace, and pure joyes;

> Kind loves keep house, ly close, and make no noise,
> And room enough for Monarchs, while none swells
> Beyond the kingdomes of contentfull Cells. (30–35)

The devotional life of Little Gidding was intense, the meals modest, the regimen of work, prayer, and praise demanding. But the self-imposed rigor of the private devotional life was, at Little Gidding, made gloriously compatible with the pronounced luxury of praising God in a public house of worship. The church was converted back from a barn into an elegant testament to the Laudian sympathies of the Ferrars. Restored in line with Laud's aims for divine worship, the church was good enough and had "room enough for Monarchs," for King Charles himself visited the retreat. New furniture was brought in, and both its value and its position within the church indicate the High Anglican temperament of the Ferrars. Peter Peckard, Nicholas Ferrar's biographer, records the changes that resulted:

The pulpit was fixed on the north, and the reading desk over against it, on the south side of the church, and both on the same level: it being thought improper that a higher place should be appointed for preaching, than that which was allotted for prayer. A new font was also provided, the leg, laver, and cover all of brass, handsomely and expensively wrought and carved; with a large brass lectern, or pillar and eagle of brass for the Bible.

He describes further the "blue taffety, and cushions of the finest tapestry and blue silk," the silver patin, chalice, and candlesticks that adorned the communion table. Understatedly, Peckard concludes that "thus was the church decently furnished, and ever after kept elegantly neat and clean."[32]

Peckard tells us that Little Gidding was regarded with some suspicion by both left and right, Puritan and Papist. But the Puritans no doubt found the community more offensive. A few years after Nicholas Ferrar's death in 1637, a treatise was addressed to Parliament entitled "The Arminian Nunnery, or a Brief Description and Relation of the newly erected Monasticall Place called the Arminian Nunnery at Little Gidding" and attacking the "Papist" features of Ferrar's community. While there is no evidence that the residents of Little Gidding were sympathetic to the Roman church, there is little doubt about the Arminian (or High Anglican) theology of the community. Furthermore, although their aim was to shun the public and political life of England in favor of a secluded existence, the Ferrars could not avoid becoming involved in the religious and political conflict enveloping the country. On at least two occasions King Charles visited Little Gidding, apparently with considerable satisfaction. In May 1633 he visited for a short time and viewed the church "with great pleasure."[33] He also requested a copy of *The Concordance* (a "harmony" of the gospels) being manufactured by the community in their trade as book binders. A year later, in a happy collocation of like-minded Royalists and Anglicans, the Ferrars sent *The Concordance* to the king in London, using Laud and Cosin as its carriers. In 1642 Charles made a hurried visit to Little Gidding and is said again to have expressed pleasure at what he saw: "Truly, this is worthy of the sight. I did not think to have seen a thing in this kind that so well pleaseth me. God's blessing be upon the founders of it."[34] In the eyes of the radical Puritans there was, for sure, no doubt about the position of Little Gidding; in 1647 the house, church, and grounds were ransacked by Parliamentary forces intent on silencing the symbolic opposition represented by the community.

Such a community was the perfect setting for the poet who would himself evoke a Ferrarian ideal: "I would be married, but I'de have no Wife,/I would be married to a single Life." Peckard describes the intimacy that, given the religious and political views of each, seems almost inevitable: "Several religious persons both in the neighbourhood, and from distant places, attended these watchings: and amongst these the celebrated Mr. Rich. Crashaw, Fellow of Peterhouse, who was very intimate in the family, and frequently came from Cambridge for this purpose, and at his return often watched in Little S. Mary's Church near Peterhouse."[35] One of Crashaw's pupils at Peterhouse was Ferrar Collet, nephew of Nicholas, and his association with the Ferrars continued even after his exile from Cambridge. The only surviving letter from Crashaw is dated February 1644 from Leyden, Holland; it is probably written to John Ferrar, brother of Nicholas, and primarily concerns two other members of the Ferrar community, Ferrar Collet and the "mother" of Little Gidding, Mary Collet.[36]

Crashaw did not, of course, have to go to Little Gidding to find political and religious sentiments he could share. They were everywhere present at Peterhouse, particularly under the direction of John Cosin, Master of Peterhouse from 1634 until his ejection by Parliament in 1644. One of Cosin's noteworthy achievements was the completion of the new chapel first begun under the Mastership of Matthew Wren. The chapel was thoroughly Laudian in all respects and thoroughly offensive to the Puritan notions of simplicity and modesty. One Puritan observer commented on the lavish appearance of the chapel and the "Popish ceremonies" there condoned, citing for particular scorn "a glorious new Altar" before which all worshipers were required to bow.[37]

The Puritan's disdain for the candlesticks, crucifix, and other religious accoutrements said to be in the chapel was obviously not shared by Crashaw, whose two Latin poems on Peterhouse reveal his enthusiasm for the new structure. The poems, written in 1635 or 1636, include requests for contributions toward the completion of the chapel, which Crashaw invokes as *"Domus* ô dulcissima rerum!"* (O sweetest *House* in the world!). In "Votiva Domus Petrensis Pro Domo Dei" (Peterhouse praying for the House of God) he visualizes the altar, vaults, floor, roof, window, and organ and urges their completion. In "Ejusdem In cætororum Operam difficili Parturitione Gemitus" (The Lamentation of the same on the difficult Labor for the rest of the work) he portrays the still incomplete Peterhouse as a "Mater" needing the honor and attention of her children.

There is a further Puritan reaction to Crashaw's role as preacher and curate that, although unquestionably biased, is likely to give an accurate portrayal of Crashaw's pleasure in the worship of the chapel and Little St. Mary's. In a document written around 1641 Puritan investigators compiled an account of the "heretical" practices at Cambridge. Coming under particular suspicion are the practices at Peterhouse, and among those specifically accused are Joseph Beaumont, Crashaw's close friend, and then Crashaw himself. Crashaw is cited for worshiping the Virgin, for engaging in "superstitious" practices at Little St. Mary's, and for following "the popish doctrine of private masses." We are also told of "other practices . . . of the like nature" which could be discovered.[38]

The High Anglican and Royalist sentiments of Peterhouse, and indeed of much of Cambridge, made conflict with Puritans and Parliament inevitable. Numerous accusations of "popish" activity during the years 1636–1644 led to growing tension and disruption, creating divisions within the university, and between the university and Parliament, that mirrored the growing religious, political, and military conflict on the outside. When Parliament decided to move against the university, it did so decisively. In August 1643 Parliament passed an ordinance requiring all chapels and churches to destroy all altars, tables of stone, tapers, crucifixes, and "all other images and pictures of saints or superstitious inscriptions."[39] On December 21, 1643, an agent of Parliament, William Dowsing, led a group of officers and soldiers to Peterhouse to execute the ordinance. While there, Dowsing relates, "we pulled down 2 mighty great Angells with Wings, & divers other Angells, & the 4 Evangelists & Peter with his Keies over the Chappell Dore, & about a hundred Chirubims & Angells & divers Superstitious Letters in gold."[40]

On February 26, 1644, the Earl of Manchester, acting as Parliamentary Commissioner, issued an order to the President of the university requiring him to instruct all Fellows, Scholars, and Officers of Peterhouse to be in residence on March 10 and to answer any charges put forth. On March 13 Cosin was expelled from his Mastership "for opposing the proceedings of Parliament, and other scandalous acts."[41] On April 8 Beaumont and Crashaw, along with three others, were formally ejected from their Fellowships for not being in residence as required.

D. Conversion and Last Years

Crashaw was not in Cambridge at the time of his ejection, and his activity from 1643–1649 can only occasionally be traced with certainty. Several documents mentioning Crashaw and dated over the last several years before the ejection proceedings confirm his Royalist and Laudian position, so he would have known that, with the increasing power of Parliamentary forces, his own situation was ever more precarious. Austin Warren suggests that he probably left Cambridge in January 1643, but the first ascertainable date is February 1644, when Crashaw wrote his letter from Leyden.[42] The poverty that will plague him during his final years is already affecting him, for a principal aim of the letter is to have Ferrar Collet, his former pupil, help him secure monetary support from the Fellowship which, in a few months, he will lose. Crashaw may have returned to England and Oxford, since during this time the king and his party were in residence there. If so, it was possibly there that he made acquaintance with the Countess of Denbigh and Queen Henrietta Maria. On September 7, 1646, the queen, writing to Pope Innocent to encourage a favorable reception of Crashaw in Rome, speaks of his having been at both English universities, a claim that may result from this occasion.[43]

We cannot be certain of the date of Crashaw's conversion to Rome, but it probably occurred in 1645. In his letter from Leyden Crashaw refers to some decision that he has been considering, but he admits to "a defect at least a disproportion of my weak soul to severer courses, I am not at present purposed for fixing."[44] It seems likely, as Martin suggests, that the decision is his imminent conversion to Rome, and his "defect" is his hesitancy in making that change.[45] The queen's 1646 letter confirms that Crashaw is at that time a convert deserving of the Pope's special attention.

Crashaw's final years were in dramatic contrast to his life at Peterhouse. He had been forced to leave the security and satisfaction of a university experience he had known for nearly twelve years. Moreover, he had made the decision, obviously a difficult one, to leave not only his motherland but his mother church as well. No doubt this produced even further estrangement, for previous allies and confidantes, such as John Cosin and the Ferrars, would have strongly opposed his decision to convert. Crashaw became a man without a home and with few friends. But his creative energies were not diminished during the period of personal misfortune. Two of the poems on St. Teresa may have been written during Crashaw's years at Cambridge, but other works of significance, including most of the hymns, come from the years 1645–1648, when Crashaw was in Paris and Rome. Furthermore, Crashaw revised many of his most important poems, a practice that continued, it appears, even during the final two years of his life.[46]

Crashaw went to Paris, perhaps following the queen, around 1645. There he drifted into poverty and was sustained partially through the support of Abraham Cowley. In November 1646 Crashaw arrived in Rome, where he was initially a resident in the Venerable English College, an institution set up as a hospice and then converted to a college for those studying for the priesthood.[47] In late 1647 or early 1648 Crashaw was appointed to the service of a Cardinal Pallotta, perhaps because of the effort of Sir Kenelm Digby, the queen's representative to the Pope, perhaps because of the cardinal's association with the College. He served the cardinal for over a year and was then appointed to the office of *beneficiatus* at Loreto in April 1649. We may speculate that Crashaw would have experienced in his new office some of the peace and satisfaction that had been difficult to find over the previous five years; he was now to serve in the church which, tradition said, was the house of the Virgin and the location in which she received the Annunciation. But this contentment was also to escape him, as he only barely arrived at Loreto before he became ill and died of a fever on August 21, 1649.

II   *The Artistic Setting*

The only edition of Crashaw's poetry published during his residence in England was the *Epigrammatum Sacrorum Liber*, and it is quite likely that he had a hand in getting that volume through the press. For his other poems three editions are most important. On June 1, 1646, there was entered on the Stationers' Register "a booke called Stepps to the Temple, sacred poems, &c, by Rich: Crashaw."[48] This edition marks the first public appearance of many of Crashaw's poems, including several that will be altered in 1648 and 1652 collections of his works. The 1646 edition also includes *The Delights of the Muses*, a gathering of secular and occasional poems. Crashaw was apparently in Paris when the volume first appeared, but the editor of the first *Steps* was probably a friend of Crashaw, and the poet may therefore have known of and possibly even supported the publication. The 1648 *Steps* includes new poems as well as expansions and alterations of poems previously printed in 1646. Although some new poems may be revived from Crashaw's Cambridge years, Martin reasonably concludes that the new poems are often truly "new" and are thus evidence of Crashaw's continuing poetic activity.[49] In 1652 the posthumous volume of *Carmen Deo Nostro* was published in Paris; it is a carefully edited collection containing, for the most part, selected (and sometimes revised) poems from 1648. Although Crashaw had been dead for three years, the text is generally a sound one and was probably seen through the press by Thomas Car, who had befriended Crashaw in Paris and who contributed two prefatory poems to it.[50]

Crashaw's reputation has depended primarily on the poems in

Carmen Deo Nostro, and, in view of this, most assessments of his overall poetic achievement conclude that he stands alone in the history of English verse, in large part because he is seen as more Continental than English, more a product of pervasive European influences than of his native English heritage—in a word, "Baroque." Thus his poetry has been called "an anomaly in English literature"; if discussed among his contemporary English Metaphysical poets, he is judged to be "the least typical"; and his achievement, if praised at all, is often thought to be a "peculiar kind of greatness."[51] Of late, we have begun to realize that Crashaw is not so peculiar, and certainly not so bizarre, as earlier commentaries tend to suggest. What appears to be an excessive, even grotesque, image is likely to have clear analogues in the literature of his day and before.

Still, there is something distinct about the poetry of Crashaw, and that quality is not explained simply in an appeal to the Baroque. Rather, we see in Crashaw a unique fusion of various theological, aesthetic, and personal forces that result in a truly eclectic art, and in this his poetry is rightly associated with the changing historical and religious climate outlined in previous pages. Seventeenth-century England, as we have seen, was a time of upheaval and transition—politically, religiously, and artistically as well. In this context, where art, however personal and private, relates to and grows out of a time of separation and synthesis, Crashaw's works are best understood. And given this broadly defined milieu, his poetry, while certainly not "typical" of the English Metaphysicals, might well be seen as more representative of his era than is usually thought to be the case. Writing after the principal achievements of the Metaphysicals Donne and Herbert, and before those of John Milton, the best-known poet of the English Baroque, Crashaw—"the one figure we may call 'Baroque' and 'Metaphysical' at once"[52]—reflects the changing character of English (and European) poetry during the time and is thus, if not a major poet, at least a significant and transitional figure in his age, more paradigmatic than "peculiar."

One of the important developments in late medieval church music was the imposition of the varied and harmonious pattern of the descant upon the straightforward melody of the plainsong, a musical embellishment that is underscored in the heading of Crashaw's paraphrase of the Latin "Stabat Mater Dolorosa" ("A

Patheticall descant upon the devout Plainsong"). Crashaw's poetry as a whole exhibits an analogous development, beginning with more simple and direct melodies and progressing toward the full range of harmony and amplification in his finest Baroque pieces. The youthful poet writes within the traditions and in the forms learned by the schoolboy, yielding examples of Spenserian floridity or Jonsonian plainness, and shows an initial capability, if not accomplishment, in a classical medium. There are, furthermore, other and more important examples of poems most profitably studied in the context of what we now know as the Metaphysical tradition, demonstrating more intellectual and more introspective verse. And there is, finally, the decisive evidence of a profound movement, especially during the last decade of Crashaw's writing, toward the sensuousness of the Baroque and the more elevated heights of religious ecstasy.[53]

These initial comments on the artistic background suggest a rough pattern of development in Crashaw's verse that associates his poetry with the Renaissance, Metaphysical (or Mannerist), and Baroque modes. Crashaw's poetry, however, not only serves as a paradigm for the progressive styles of the seventeenth century; more importantly, and somewhat contradictorily, his poetry confirms the particular confluence of styles during this period and argues for the inadequacy of strict poetic categories. Crashaw's poetry may well be the best evidence that the first half of the seventeenth century was not only a time of change in artistic styles but a time of integration as well. In a remarkable number of poems, particularly those from his mature years, he demonstrates the truth of Louis Martz's observation that "the phases of style that we call Renaissance, Mannerist, or Baroque all flow together and in England become inseparably intermingled and simultaneous."[54]

A.   Renaissance Classicism

The virtues of Renaissance classicism are its order, its sense of balance and proportion, its attainment of a decorous beauty through a fit harmony of subject and verse. Wylie Sypher asserts that the "renaissance composition" is one in which the Renaissance painter and poet "created a formal domain of Beauty regulated by algebraic equations and platonic notions of harmony." Thus, the measures of achievement in Renaissance art and literature reinforce the Renaissance "notion of harmonious proportion, ideal ratios, and the coherent 'realization' of a scene or action from a fixed point of view."[55] In late sixteenth- and early seventeenth-century England two dominant modes of classicism emerged. The one stressed regularity in form and decorum in subject, but embellished art with flowery language, decorative imagery, and frequent allusions (usually from classical myths), and thus sacrificed directness and plainness for the beauty of ornamentation and the sweetness of style. The other version of the tradition emphasized plainness and directness, eschewing both ornamentation and intellectual complexity to realize the more modest, but no less compelling, achievements of a plain style. These are, in brief, the traditions we associate most with Spenser and Jonson, and we see some few poems in which Crashaw follows each.

Crashaw's ability to write in the vein of Spenser and other Elizabethans is evident in several early poems, notably those on the king's coronation and the various members of the royal family. The middle of one of the odes titled "Upon the Kings Coronation" ("Strange Metamorphosis!") might have come out of the late sixteenth century:

> Amazed Sol throwes of his mournfull weeds,
> Speedily harnessing his fiery steeds,
> Up to Olympus stately topp he hies,
> From whence his glorious rivall hee espies. (15–18)

Imagery and effects such as this lead Warren to observe that "books, pictures, and music [were] the normal stimuli to [Crashaw's] composition."[56] The royal poems as a group introduce us to the mellifluous style of the Spenserians—inflated, bookish, often allegorical in mode.

Flowery language and classical allusions are also evident in "Upon the Death of Mr. Herrys," and the poem sometimes reads like a pale imitation of Spenser. Herrys before his death is seen as a "Plant of noble stemme" and his growth is couched in terms that are so much a part of the Spenserian tradition that they would otherwise defy precise attribution. "The Morning Muses perch like Birds" on his branches, and the "purest Pearles" of dew rest on his leaves:

> The balmy *Zephirus* got so sweet a Breath
> By often kissing them. And now begun
> Glad Time to ripen expectation. (20–22)[56a]

A plainer classicism is evident in "To the Morning. Satisfaction
for sleepe." It too contains allusions to Aurora, Morpheus, Apollo,
Lethe, and Helicon, but the subject is more personal and the style
more direct. Classical references are uttered with a poetic tongue
in cheek; they are not taken seriously as they are in the coronation
poems. Crashaw's plain style is also apparent in some of his elegies.
His "Epitaph Upon Mr. Ashton" is simple and unpretentious, a
poem whose virtues befit the grace and modest achievements of its
subject. Crashaw's Latin text for the memorial tablet of William
Herrys reflects a classical emphasis on balance, proportion, and
directness, and in its decisive rhetorical parallelism it manifests the
Renaissance ideals of order and harmony of parts. The finest
example of the plain style in Crashaw is "Wishes. To his (supposed)
Mistresse," a poem compact and controlled in structure, subdued
and effective in imagery. The qualities wished for are described in
turn, but there is little of the kind of extension and elaboration
evident in some of Crashaw's more Baroque pieces:

> Smiles, that can warme
> The blood, yet teach a charme,
> That Chastity shall take no harme.
>
> Blushes, that bin
> The burnish of no sin,
> Nor flames of ought too hot within.
>
> Joyes, that confesse,
> Vertue their Mistresse,
> And have no other head to dresse. (61–69)

There are, finally, the numerous examples from Crashaw's Latin
and English epigrams that reveal the directness of a poetic
"plainsong." The Latin language and the strict epigrammatic form
necessitate a more direct style, of course, and thus generalizations
based on the epigrams are problematic. Nonetheless, these poems
without doubt often stand apart from the lush and sensuous quality
of the Baroque. And it is additionally significant that Crashaw's
achievement within this structurally confining medium, so opposite from the expansiveness of the Baroque, is unsurpassed among
English poets. Exhibiting a strictness of form, style, and statement
that we associate with the Renaissance mode, the epigrams reveal

even more profoundly the wit, intellectuality, and dramatic character that recall the Metaphysical mode. Crashaw's poems following the Renaissance tradition are few and modest, but his place among the Metaphysical poets, though surely distinct, is significant and enduring.

B. The Metaphysical Tradition

One of the problems attaching to discussions of Metaphysical poetry has been the temptation to define it too simply in terms of the poetry of Donne—although that is a limitation several recent studies have avoided.[57] With Donne as the standard, poets who move away from his model are thought to move away from the Metaphysical tradition itself. This correlation is evident in discussions of Crashaw's Metaphysical traits, for virtually all who mention him in that context end up qualifying their judgments markedly. By contrasting him with Marino, Vondel, or Giles Fletcher, Frank Warnke concludes that Crashaw is "clearly Metaphysical" and is a poet who "is ultimately faithful to the native Metaphysical tradition." But he later admits that "we consider Crashaw the least typical of the English Metaphysicals." Earl Miner finds that "the things that give Donne's poetry much of its drive"—the strong satirical element, the sense of personal antagonism, the tension resulting from a balance of opposites—"are either absent or transformed in [Crashaw's] best-known poetry." Joan Bennett, discussing Crashaw as one of her *Five Metaphysical Poets*, nonetheless admits that he seems "to fit uneasily" into an account of the Metaphysical tradition; she later observes that "it is doubtful whether a poet in whom the senses and the emotions were so much more active than the intellect, was well served by the metaphysical style." Douglas Bush states the case most emphatically: "If the chief stigmata of the metaphysical poet, according to modern definitions, are inward conflict and tension, philosophic and analytic complexity of mind, and a colloquial, realistic, and non-pictorial manner and texture, Crashaw was something else."[58]

It is perhaps beyond argument that Crashaw was, finally, "something else," and he does, no doubt, "fit uneasily" into a study of Metaphysical poets, but that fact ought not to prevent our perception of the significant elements of the Metaphysical tradition that recur in Crashaw's poetry. To begin with, a number of poems provide specific evidence of the decisive influence of the Metaphysical style on the development of Crashaw's verse.

"Death's Lecture" is perhaps the most Metaphysical of Crashaw's poems in style: analytical and satirical in attitude, abrupt and antimelodic in meter, Donnean in imagery. Humankind is seen in bitter and unflattering terms, as "Hyperbolized NOTHING" and as "Huge emptynes." The tone of the poem is particularly reminiscent of Donne's *Anniversaries*, as humanity is urged to look on itself to see its own worthlessness, its "neighbourhood to NOTHING." In "Temperance" ("Upon the Translation of Lessius") two different images are Metaphysical in both the literary and the philosophical sense of the term, using a familiar experience to clarify a spiritual one through a Metaphysical conceit. The ability of the soul to be revealed brilliantly through the body is likened to a veil that at once covers and reveals the beauty of a face:

> A soul sheath'd in a christall shrine;
> Through which all her bright features shine;
> As when a peice of wanton lawn
> A thinne, aeriall veil, is drawn
> Or'e beauty's face; seeming to hide
> More sweetly showes the blushing bride. (23-28)

When soul and body must part, death is seen as the gentle parting of friends: "Soul & body part like freinds;/No quarrells, murmurs, no delay;/A KISSE, a SIGH, and so away" (48-50).

Two of the elegies on the death of William Herrys, "Upon the Death of the most desired Mr. Herrys" and "Another," are alike in their tough-minded response to death, and in style and technique each poem reveals the further influence of the Metaphysical tradition. The abrupt opening of the first poem,

> Death, what dost? ô hold thy Blow,
> What thou dost, thou dost not know,

recalls the numerous examples from Donne and Herbert of a similar attempt to shock or arouse immediate interest through a dramatic opening. The second poem echoes Donne's haunting refrain in his *Anniversaries* ("Shee, shee is dead; shee's dead") with its equally plaintive cry over the death of a friend: "But he, alas! even hee is dead." In differing ways other poems reveal Crashaw's continuing association with the Metaphysical tradition, from the logical structure and Donne-like title of "Loves Horoscope" to the Herbert-like quality of "Charitas Nimia" and "Office of the Holy Crosse" to the personal and dramatic note struck at times in the hymns and in the 1652 poem to the Countess of Denbigh.

Enough examples could be presented to make a convincing case for Crashaw's use of particular elements of the Metaphysical style, but the importance of this artistic context goes much further. Metaphysical poetry ultimately derives from a particular vision of the world, and it is this vision that Crashaw, however much he may at times work through his own unique style, shares with his contemporary Metaphysicals. Metaphysical verse is driven "by an overwhelming concern with metaphysical problems; with problems either deriving from or closely resembling, in the nature of their difficulty, the problem of the Many and the One."[59] Metaphysical poets use imagery seriously, not lightly or decoratively, to work through their metaphysical problem; the imagery is analytical and intellectual, having as its fundamental aim a synthesis, often achieved through paradox, of varied or conflicting moments of experience. The perception of contradictions or paradoxes in the very nature of things—what one critic has called the "metaphysical note"[60]—and the resulting attempt to unify and resolve those contradictions is evident in Donne's conjunction of human and divine love and in Herbert's use of familiar and colloquial imagery in sacred verse. Crashaw's poetry often realizes a similar effect, as he brings to his sacred verse such varied moods as frivolity, shock, and condescension and responds to the theological question before him with a heightened sense of paradox.

The attempt of the Metaphysical poet to unify experience is seen most concretely in the Metaphysical conceit, that particular intellectual conjunction of two separated but somehow linked occasions or things. Samuel Johnson was wrong only in his negative attitude when he cited the Metaphysical habit of yoking heterogeneous ideas together with violence and of straining after the new or unusual or pursuing a thought or image to its farthest point.[61] That poetic aim to establish correspondences is based, as Joseph Mazzeo has shown, on a profound sense of universal correspondences and analogies in the world itself.[62] God is seen as a superior "metaphysical" poet with the created world as His poem, giving divine sanction to the seventeenth-century poet's aim to associate and unify experiences through the conceit: "The universe is a vast net of correspondences which unites the whole multiplicity of being. The poet approaches and creates his reality by a series of more or less elaborate correspondences."[63]

Because the attempt to unify and synthesize experience means joining seemingly unrelated moments, the poet must rely on his ingenuity and wit (*arguzia*). The two prominent catchwords of Metaphysical poetry, conceit and wit, are thus intricately related characteristics descriptive of the poet's attempts to concretize and synthesize his subjects. A sense of correspondences and analogies results in the poetic image of the conceit, which in turn can often be accomplished only through the thoughtful and witty poetic act of joining on the part of the poet. Thus, human is joined with divine, abstract with concrete, religious with erotic, commonplace with sacred, in images that are at once far-fetched and profound.[64] This unifying aim is, as noted before, a basis for the prominence of paradox in Metaphysical verse since paradox holds in balance and intellectually unifies contradictory truths. On a theological level the paradox is represented in, and divinely sanctioned by, the Incarnation, where God becoming human acts as the ultimate example of a profound metaphysical wit. The Incarnation, viewed from the perspective of a poet such as Crashaw, is the consummate fusion of humanity and God, sin and perfection, emotion and intellect, and is as well the essential model for this synthesizing mode, for what has been termed the "central impulse" of Metaphysical poets: "to view emotional experience in terms of its implicit metaphysical and theological mysteries."[65]

These features definitive of the Metaphysical tradition—the sense of profound universal analogies, the prominence of wit and paradox, a logical and analytical capacity—play at times a significant role in Crashaw's poetry. No doubt they are, as Earl Miner puts it, often "transformed" in the hands of Crashaw, particularly as they meet the increasingly Baroque and sensuous quality of his later verse. But the transformation, although crucial and distinct, does not negate the Metaphysical connection in much of Crashaw's poetry. The logical and intellectual element of his poetry has been too easily dismissed, largely because the best-known poems give such full reign to the senses. But in most of these poems, even those thought to be essentially Baroque, there is a logical structure and pattern of development that comes from a poet who was capably served by the intellectual emphasis of the Metaphysical tradition.

In contrast to the limited influence of the Renaissance mode, the Metaphysical tradition is more pervasive in Crashaw's verse, and it thus plays a continuing role, especially during the middle writing stages, in the development of his poetry. The 1646 edition of *Steps to the Temple* opens with the "motto" of the poet whose longer sacred works are there presented for the first time: "Live, Jesus, Live, and let it bee/My life to dye, for love of thee."[66] The *terminus* of the 1652 *Carmen Deo Nostro* recalls that motto in a Latin phrase, "VIVE JESU" (Live Jesus). The emphasis on a life whose meaning is defined through paradox is thus given a formal prominence that encloses Crashaw's most significant works; furthermore, we see in the poetry a constant recognition of the metaphysical implications of this perception of life.

The most profound characteristic integral to the Metaphysical vision is also the most persistent feature of Crashaw's poetry, from early to late: Crashaw's fascination with the Incarnation aligns him with the Metaphysical tradition as no other characteristic does, and the poems in which the Incarnation occupies a thematic and theological center range from the earliest epigrams to the later and grander hymns on the Epiphany and the Nativity. No single description adequately defines Crashaw's poetic use of the Incarnation, for he responds with rich variety of emotion and technique. At times the "implicit metaphysical and theological mysteries" in the Incarnation are muted by a more Baroque Crashaw who dwells on the "emotional experience" of the moment—the soft and innocent babe, the warm and nourishing mother—or who states and restates the essential theological mysteries with a sense of excitement and awe, as in the Nativity Hymn. But Crashaw is also capable of realizing paradox, both within and outside the Incarnation, through a significant intellectual effort. Numerous early and youthful epigrams testify to the wit and ingenuity necessary both to see and to create paradox; near the opposite end of his life and his poetic activity, the Epiphany Hymn works through multiple mysteries with a style and a complexity of theme and imagery that places the poem firmly within the Metaphysical tradition. The Epiphany Hymn is, in several ways, distinct among Crashaw's poems, and it would be wrong to suggest otherwise. But the poem is certain evidence that Crashaw, though moving beyond the

Metaphysical tradition in style and technique, nonetheless remains profoundly "metaphysical" to the end.

C. Baroque Sensibility

In reading Crashaw we realize that, while often Metaphysical in quality, his poetry, especially the later verse, is often more than Metaphysical. It is as if one tradition has been superimposed on another, one harmonic line played over another and thus partially, but by no means entirely, masking the first. The Baroque mode gains this kind of dominance in Crashaw's later verse, but we should not forget that the two traditions, although characteristically divergent in emphasis, may also work simultaneously. A Crashaw poem may indeed be both "'Baroque' and 'Metaphysical' at once."

The progression from Metaphysical to Baroque may be, from a larger perspective, part of the natural rhythm of the creative arts, the systole and diastole between a more classical mode and some form of anticlassicism: thus, Renaissance leads to Metaphysical or Mannerism, Neo-Classicism to Romanticism, Victorian to Modern.[67] In this view, the development from Metaphysical to Baroque is a change from a less to a more classical form, although the Baroque is clearly classicism with something extra.

Metaphysical literature is characterized by an intellectual emphasis and by a synthesis of thought and feeling through an active engagement of the mind on a metaphysical problem. Baroque art revels in the emotions and senses; the intellectual element is muted in order to let the exuberance, energy, and decoration of the poetry come triumphantly through. The Metaphysical mode results in a more "cerebral and paradoxical art," while Baroque art "is highly sensuous in its imagery but phantasmagoric rather than representational in the effects created by the imagery."[68] While imagery is prominent in both, the purposes and effects of the imagery vary. The Metaphysical conceit is a manifestation of the perception of correspondences and analogies governing a seventeenth-century vision of the world and is thus a concise and witty emblem of that metaphysical vision. The Baroque conceit is more ornamental, is often repeated and reviewed, and finally serves a more emotive end: "the Baroque conceit does not explore: it rather views the same paradox or symbol from various angles, reviewing and revising and restating and expanding the issue until some truth of emotion gradually grows out from all that glittering elaboration."[69]

Baroque art is more decorative than its Metaphysical counterpart, and in this feature we can see Baroque art as a revival of Renaissance art rather than a turning from it. The use of ornamental imagery is reminiscent of the lush imagery of Spenser and the Elizabethan sonneteers and creates "a style which is more a hyperextension of Renaissance techniques than a revolt against these techniques."[70] While the Metaphysical strain and the Metaphysical conceit grow out of a sense of conflict, tension, and paradox yielding to resolution through an intellectual synthesis, the Baroque response is not resolution through metaphysical unity so much as resolution through assertion and ornamentation. It is an art that chooses "to resolve all doubts in splendor."[71]

Baroque art is, fundamentally, "an art given to superlatives."[72] It is, relative to Renaissance and Metaphysical verse, characterized by abundance and overstatement or, in a more negative sense, by excess and extravagance. Baroque art is true to its Renaissance heritage in having order and control, but it goes beyond its heritage by testing that control to its utmost. It is art that is very nearly bursting its seams or escaping its harmonic line, but it does not do so. This prominence of "l'abondance et désordonnée" leads at times to excess, to a too-conscious attempt at the luxurious, the triumphant, the grand.[73] Marino's dictum that the aim of the poet is the marvelous "È del poeta il fin la meraviglia") yields, in the hands of clumsy artisans, to embarrassing sensationalism and sentimentality. But in the best hands it is fashioned into an art that is intense, energetic, and powerful, that works through its control and symmetry to realize the "violent aspiration of the Baroque spirit" and to give vent to the "daring cast of imagination" that characterizes Baroque achievement.[74] In its aim to assert its own magnificence, Baroque art reaches to the very heights of the nature and strivings of humankind.

The principal poems from *Carmen Deo Nostro* illustrate these qualities of energy, abundance, sensuousness, and, indeed, an abundant sensuousness. Particularly in the poems on or addressed to various women and in his major hymns Crashaw evokes the senses with thoroughness and exuberance. His own "daring cast of imagination" is most apparent in his energetic pursuit of the truths of divine love by consistently viewing it in terms of its earthly

counterpart. Thus St. Teresa is seen, in overtly sensual terms, as the
ecstatic recipient of the love of Christ, and other women are
similarly urged to accept divine love in language that evokes the
physical senses. At the close of the Ode on a Prayer Book, for
example, the woman addressed ("Mrs. M.R.") is reminded of the
abundance of God's love ("Boundles and infinite/Bottomles
treasures/Of pure inebriating pleasures") and is invited to accept
the role of God's chosen mate: "Happy proof! she shal discover/
What joy, what blisse,/How many Heav'ns at once it is/To have
her GOD become her LOVER."

Baroque abundance is also seen on a more concrete and stylistic
level in the tendency toward repetition—of words and phrases but
also of similar or identical images. It is not so much that the same
word or phrase or image is repeated verbatim but that the
controlling idea governing each is viewed repeatedly from different perspectives. We find, for example, that Crashaw's total poetic
vocabulary is rather small, in part because his favorite words—
"sweet," "heaven," "fair," "life," "great," "breast," "soul"—recur
throughout the canon. Furthermore, even in his use of rhyme,
Crashaw tends toward a repetition of favorite rhyming combina-
tions.[75] A Baroque poet often lingers over a sound or image, repeats
it, or views it anew with slight change. The Metaphysical conceit is
often concise, but even if extended it is ordinarily explored
through logical or analogical analysis before the poet moves on to
other concerns. A "repetition of conceit" governs the imagery of
the typical Baroque poet.[76] Hence, a poem like Crashaw's "The
Weeper" seems to move slowly through its stanzas, as a reader is
forced to dwell on images that sound very much like one another.
Repetition gives the impression of plenitude and elaboration
though it may not be true elaboration at all. As a consciously
rhetorical strategy, it demonstrates the Baroque artists' desire to
exhaust the emotional and spiritual content of their material—to
view it and review it until that desired "truth of emotion gradually
grows out from all that glittering elaboration."

A further point will enhance our understanding of the Baroque
quality of Crashaw's verse. Metaphysical poetry emphasizes the
self and is largely an intense drama about the self. In this context,
we realize that the Baroque quality of Crashaw at times takes him
farthest from his contemporary Metaphysical poets. For in some
notable works his is not only a Baroque art but also a mystical art.

Particularly under the influence of St. Teresa and, possibly, other Spanish mystics, Crashaw strove for an achievement that would ultimately deny rather than affirm the self. At the close of his third poem on St. Teresa, "The Flaming Heart," in lines addressed to the saint, the poet seeks the death of self in an affirmation of a universal absolute—mystical union with the deity:

> By all of HIM we have in THEE;
> Leave nothing of my SELF in me.
> Let me so read thy life, that I
> Unto all life of mine may dy. (105–108)

Mysticism leads to a denial of the phenomenal world and to a deemphasis on the human being experiencing the vision or writing the poem. While Crashaw uses sensuous conceits, his ultimate aim is to assert the superiority of a spiritual world greater than that of a world of the senses. It is as if the ecstasy of the spiritual world can be approached, imaginatively, only through the luxuriousness of the senses, but the aim is both to use sense imagery in all its richness and to deny the ultimate value of a sensible and physically limited world. Thus in the finest of Crashaw's Baroque verse "the rich excess of sensuous imagery and the passionate expression of quasi-sexual emotion end in the affirmation of their opposite—the exclusive reality of the world of the spirit."[77] What Laudian and Roman churches sought to do in their cathedrals, Crashaw strove to achieve in his Baroque verse—the realization of God through luxury.

Frank Warnke has identified one of the basic tensions typical of Metaphysical poetry as "that which exists between . . . a full-blooded conception of character and . . . the soul's desire to lose its identity in some all-embracing unity, whether the unity of sexual love or that of God. From the hard and disturbing interplay of self-awareness and aspiration this poetry derives its dialectic and its enduring value."[78] The description is most fitting for Donne, in both his secular and his sacred poetry. All of the elements are present in that delicately maintained balance and tension so definitive of Metaphysical verse. For the Baroque Crashaw the tension, at least this kind of tension, is largely gone. The "full-blooded conception of character" is very nearly overwhelmed by "the soul's desire to lose its identity," and "self-awareness" gives way to aspiration and flight. As Earl Miner observes, in poems of this type, Crashaw "seems to have difficulty in touching earth."[79]

Since Austin Warren's seminal study of the "Baroque sensibility" of Crashaw there has been little quarrel with the accuracy of that poetic label; Douglas Bush carries it to its furthest extreme by asserting that the simplest definition of the Baroque is "poetry like Crashaw's."[80] Bush's statement is, however, necessarily misleading, for he clearly has particular poems in mind, those that best exemplify the qualities he associates most with the Baroque—"Musicks Duell," "The Weeper," and the Teresa poems, perhaps. The varied traditions outlined in this chapter suggest a need for approaching Crashaw's works without any overt critical bias. To do so is not to negate the stature of Crashaw as a Baroque poet but to recognize greater scope to his work. The following chapters will demonstrate, I believe, the value of understanding more acutely the development of Crashaw's style and poetic sensibility if we intend to appreciate his works, from early to late, and to accept the varying aims and themes of poems that on occasion differ quite markedly from one another.

CHAPTER 2

Apprenticeship: The Epigrams and Early Translations

I The Epigrams

WHEN the young Richard Crashaw entered the Charterhouse school at the age of sixteen or seventeen, he encountered a disciplined and traditional program that proved invaluable as a training ground for his developing talents as a poet. Charterhouse, like other grammar schools of the time, incorporated classical instruction as the backbone of its course of study, the genesis of which was the medieval curriculum of the seven liberal arts: the trivium (logic, grammar, and rhetoric) and the quadrivium (music, arithmetic, geometry, and astronomy). Hence, students at Charterhouse were expected to read widely in classical authors, to copy notes and phrases from those authors for future use, and to "imitate" classical authors in their own compositions.

Crashaw participated in an even more exciting regimen regarding one form of poetic "composition": the epigram. At Charterhouse he benefited from the instruction of the Master, Robert Brooke, and as a result, according to Lloyd, "his own pretty conceits [were] improved by those of the choicest Orators and Poets, which he was not onely taught to understand, but imitate and make, not only their rich sense his own, but to smooth his soul as well as fill it."[1] Writing epigrams in imitation of classical authors was a practice frequently taught by schools and colleges of the early seventeenth century, and for good reason; epigrams were short pieces, rigorous in form and yet exhibiting a variety both of subjects and of rhetorical devices that could later be put to good use in more mature or more extended works.[2] We know, furthermore, that at Charterhouse Crashaw very likely had to fulfill the requirements governing Foundation Scholars, including the provision that "they of the Highest Form shall every *Sunday* set up in the Great Hall four *Greek* and four *Latin* Verses a-piece, upon any Part of the Second Lesson appointed for that Day, for the Master of the Hospital, or any Stranger to view and examine."[3] It seems reasonable to conclude that some of Crashaw's existing epigrams may have been written during his Charterhouse years and that they may, indeed, have been a positive influence toward his acceptance at Pembroke College.

Crashaw's duties as a Scholar of the Watt Foundation at Pembroke meant that he continued to write epigrams on request or under obligation, and there is, on the surface, little reason to expect that the products of this "forced" writing should be particularly interesting or original. All schoolboys in similar positions participated in the same drills and exercises, and the results are predictably inconsequential in most instances. Furthermore, as J. W. Binns has pointed out, the very process of "poeticizing" in Latin is not encouraging to the creation of distinct verse:

A poet is likely to be less able to mould the Latin language into a new style, less able to stamp the impress of his personality on his verse, less able to shake himself free from the weight of the past as it pressed upon him with the marmoreal perfection of the Latin language. The cluster of poetic commonplaces and modes of expression, the conventional themes, instilled by the processes of education, by school grammars and florilegia, all these are liable to circumscribe the poet as he searches for the words of his poem.[4]

Given these historical and poetic facts, it is all the more remarkable that Crashaw's Latin epigrams, written almost entirely during his school and college years, are an impressive and important achievement. "He alone of the numerous English poets who must have been similarly drilled," observes Ruth Wallerstein, "created anything of importance in the mode, or felt it as an abiding influence."[5] Austin Warren's similar evaluation in his seminal study of Crashaw has gone largely unchallenged: "Distinguished of style they are: the best Latin epigrams written by an Englishman. Nor will a diligent search through the neglected volumes of Renaissance Neo-Latinity discover any master of whom Crashaw is not peer."[6]

A. The Epigrammatic Tradition

The ancestors of Crashaw's epigrams are many, including the renowned *Greek Anthology*, the various classical Latin epigrammatists, especially Martial, numerous collections of epigrams and emblems available to the reader of Crashaw's day, and, perhaps most important for Crashaw, the work of several Jesuit epigrammatists, including Jacob Bidermann, François Remond, and Bernardus Bauhusius. Among these precedents two stand out, Martial and the Jesuit epigrammatists. Martial is not so much a specific source as a pervasive influence over all epigrammatists of the Renaissance and seventeenth century; indeed, the brief, witty quality of his poems and their frequent satirical bent provided the model, and virtually the definition, for future writers of the form.[7] While, like all Renaissance epigrammatists, Crashaw felt the influence of Martial, his "real models" were the writings of the Jesuits.[8] The variety and virtuosity revealed in these highly rhetorical epigrams are similarly evident in Crashaw's poems, and the rhetorical designs so prominent in Jesuitical poetry are notable in Crashaw as well: "a highly sophisticated rhetoric of schemes and tropes, figures verbal and conceptual: parison, paromoion, polyptoton, homoeoteleuton, alliteration; the apostrophe, the rhetorical question, antithesis, personification, metaphor."[9]

Foremost among those qualities usually judged definitive for the epigram is wit (*arguzia*), and more exactly, wit in brief form. Epigrams are ordinarily brief (most of Crashaw's include two paired distichs, a total of four lines) and reach a witty, satirical, or surprising conclusion. Götthold Lessing's analysis of the epigram emphasizes its two parts and is relevant to the form and movement of a typical Crashaw epigram: the epigram first invites our "expectation" or "anticipation," then arrives promptly at a "disclosure" or "explanation."[10] Among Renaissance commentators, Scaliger, whose extensive observations on the epigram in his *Poetices libri Septem* (1561) are a particularly instructive source, stresses the characteristic brevity of the epigram and both its "witty soul" and its "witty form" (Brevitas proprium quiddam est. Argutia anima, ac quasi forma").[11] Puttenham underscores even more emphatically the tone and aim of the epigram, associating it with "taunting" and "scoffing" and describing it as a poem in which "every mery conceited man might . . . make his friend sport, and anger his foe, and give a prettie nip, or shew a sharp conceit in few verses."[12] Crashaw's epigrams in general exhibit the qualities identified above: the dominant two-part structure, the interrelationship of brevity and wit, the importance of tone; even more exactly they reflect the very aims described by Puttenham, both the "sporting" apostrophes made to "friends" (the epigrams addressed variously to the apostles, or Jesus, or Mary) and the more bitter taunts to foes (the sinners of many types and names whom Crashaw so frequently chastizes).

The quality of wit not only informed the very nature of the epigram; it also put the poet in the position of imitating God, who was deemed the ultimate source of wit. Emmanuele Tesauro (1591–1675) described thunderbolts as "formidable Witticisms" and God as a "witty speaker, who, talking in riddles to Men and Angels, clothed his most exalted concepts with various heroical Devices, and pictorial Symbols."[13] It is not surprising, therefore, that among seventeenth-century epigrammatists, everything "was subservient to wit."[14] While the poet's wit might become an end in itself, the ideal was to realize in a sacred poem a model of the truths created and revealed by God. A poet who created metaphorical and metaphysical relationships within a poem was also pointing, by analogical extension, to the more profound relationships in the universe of God's creation. Searching for pun or paradox was more than a literary or intellectual exercise; it provided insight into the paradoxes of life and of divine revelation. For Christian poets the paradox of the Incarnation provided ample justification for their own creative revelation of apparent impossibilities nonetheless meaningful to them and their audience. Even the pun, the apparently superficial play on words, could be more than a clever way of pointing to verbal similarities; as Father Walter Ong has observed, puns can be "used where semantic coincidence penetrates to startling relations in the real order of things."[15]

B.   *Epigrammatum Sacrorum Liber*

Epigrammatum Sacrorum Liber was published in 1634 with a total of 178 Latin epigrams; in addition, sixty-two Crashaw epigrams are collected in a manuscript in the Bodleian Library (Tanner MS 465) and a final three Latin epigrams (along with Crashaw's only extant Greek epigrams) are printed in the second edition of *Poemata et Epigrammata* (1670). There are, to complete the corpus, English counterparts for one-fifth of the Latin verses. To put it another way, there are Latin counterparts for all but three of the English epigrams, while the decided majority of Latin epigrams exist in one version only. That fact, and the later (1646) publication of the English or Divine Epigrams in *Steps to the Temple*, lead to the reasonable conclusion that the Latin epigrams are the originals.

For many years the rationale for the order of the Latin epigrams as they appear both in print and in manuscript was in doubt. They follow no thematic arrangement, nor are they patterned after any particular biblical or chronological sequence. The apparently fortuitous order led an early editor and translator to conclude that "the Epigrams seem to have been composed and written down on the spur of the moment as a subject struck him, and hence there is [an] absence of arrangement."[16] We can now be assured, following the work of Warren, Milhaupt, and Larsen, that the basis for the order of the poems in *Epigrammatum Sacrorum Liber* and in Tanner is the sequence of readings assigned from the Anglican *Book of Common Prayer* during the years 1631–1635.[17]

Because the topics for Crashaw's epigrams were thus, in a sense, assigned, we must be cautious in making far-reaching conclusions about what they suggest of the personal temperament or theological bias of the young poet. Nonetheless, since the readings for a given week or day offered some variety, we can make some tentative judgments about the poetic and religious inclinations revealed in Crashaw's choices. In the first place, Crashaw shows no interest in Old Testament subjects although he presumably could have based at least some of his epigrams on Old Testament readings. In this, Crashaw's sensibilities seem already inclined toward the preferred subjects of Laudian Anglicanism. The Puritan viewpoint was grounded on the Old Testament, which stresses God's selection of His chosen people and which recognizes time and again the importance of faith. God the Father demands obedience and punishes wrongdoers quickly and harshly. The High Anglican devotee was attracted to the New Testament, where the Incarnation provides the model for love and mercy and where the Christian is reassured of God's care and attention. God the Son offers Himself in love and provides the hope for salvation even for the weakest of sinners.[18] Furthermore, most of the epigrams deal with the life and death of Jesus; fewer than forty focus on apostles or other followers of Christ. Reading the epigrams as a whole we are struck by their repeated attention to the central fact and theme of Christianity: the Incarnation. The Incarnation is important throughout the epigrams both because it is to the Christian the central event in history and thus the model for all action and thought, and because it is the basis for Crashaw's unyielding attention to the paradoxical moment. For Crashaw, the Incarnation yields both subject and technique.

Let me now cite a representative Crashaw epigram. It is not necessarily his best, but it includes a number of elements that distinguish his epigrammatic style. The epigram is derived from the reading for Matins on September 8, 1633 (Matt. 9), and is headed "In cæcos Christum confitentes, Pharisæos abnegantes" (#174):

> Ne mihi, tu (Pharisæe ferox) tua lumina jactes:
> En cæcus! Christum cæcus at ille videt.

> Tu (Pharisæe) nequis in Christo cernere Christum:
> Ille videt cæcus; cæcus es ipse videns.[19]

> (You, defiant Pharisee, do not cast your eyes on me:
> See the blind man! Blind, but he sees Christ.

> You, Pharisee, are not able to see Christ in Christ:
> He sees though blind; you are blind though seeing.)

The paradox here is, of course, a familiar one in literature, and the poem as a whole offers only a few surprises. Nonetheless, we see several characteristics prominent throughout the body of Crashaw's epigrams. These include: (1) the ironic pose of the speaker; (2) the apostrophe, usually to a sinner or antagonist of Christ (but several times to Christ Himself or one of the apostles); (3) repetition (here of words ["cæcus" and "videt/videns"] and elsewhere of phrases and even sentences); (4) juxtaposition (of reactions, of events, of two persons); (5) pun and word play (here playing on the two senses of "Christ"—the anointed Messiah and the person Jesus); and (6) paradox (the blind seeing, the seeing blinded). To these I would add another not displayed here: the frequent use of interrogatives, directed sometimes to apostrophized biblical persons and sometimes asked rhetorically.

The complexity of the epigrams is characteristically enhanced by the interaction of the various techniques isolated above. In the poem just cited the poet takes on the role of one who must endure and rebut the harsh glances of those Pharisees who look askance at the action of Christ and thus implicitly deny that He *is* the Christ. He sees their defiant looks (their sight) as a sign of their denial ("abnegantes") and hence of their blindness. It is not merely, as the conventional paradox has it, that they are blind while seeing; their very sight—or more specifically the *way* they see—is the proof of their blindness. Juxtaposing the two responses allows the more effective repetition of the images and words related to blindness and seeing ("cæcus" and "videt") and leads to the consummate paradox of the poem. All the while the tone and pose are those of a superior observer commenting sarcastically on what he sees.

The persona of Crashaw's epigrams is typically one who uses irony, sarcasm, paradox—virtually anything at his disposal—to subjugate his enemies or encourage his allies. Crashaw can be straightforward in his response to a situation, but he is more often consciously playing a role to fit his purpose. In an epigram alluding to Satan's temptations of Christ, Satan feigns disbelief in Christ's power by urging Him to cast Himself down from the temple; the poet reminds Satan that Christ casts him down from the heart of man: "heus tu,/Non credes quòd sit Filius ille Dei?" (#125. There now, do you not believe that He is the Son of God?). In another example, those who hover over and make noise around a dead girl are accused of being empty-headed ("Vani") because they do not know that only Christ's whispers can awaken her (#172). Thomas's request to touch the wounds of Christ makes him a cruel man ("truculente") who, in order to believe, would make Christ suffer even more by reliving the agony of His death through Thomas's touch (#284). A poem addressed to Pilate reminds him that water can wash his hands but not his sin; only the water of his tears can have such cleansing power (#265). Those who are condemned for confessing Christ (John 9:22) are seen by the poet with playful irony as unfortunate defendants ("reus infelix") because for that confession they will be "condemned" ("damnabere") to heaven (#203). In a witty and effective jab at Peter, the poet accuses the apostle of cutting off the ear of the soldier in Gethsemane in order to have one less witness to his later denial of the very Christ he proposes to defend (#262).

As these selections indicate, the ironic pose of the speaker is

often based on the fact that the persons addressed or described in
the poem are shown in a weak or sinful state, and the poet thus
attempts to instruct or indict through wit and irony. A number of
poems are addressed to Christ or the faithful, but more significantly the poems expose the sins of the faithless—the unbelieving
Jews (#s 137, 299, 234), Pilate (#s 265, 266), Agrippa (#321), or the
Pharisees (#s 132, 240, 174, 221, 237). Even the closest followers of
Christ are often seen in moments of weakness: Thomas as he insists
on touching Christ's wounds (#s 284, 285), Peter as he cuts off the
ear of the soldier or sinks into the sea because of weak faith (#180)
or denies Christ (#248), James and John as they seek a special place
in heaven (#224).

Three of the qualities isolated earlier—the ironic pose, the
apostrophe, the interrogatives—are related fundamentally to the
role of the speaker and his association with an implicit audience. In
a poem addressed to the prodigal son we see each of these features
prominently. The poem is headed "Congestis omnibus peregrè
profectus est" and is taken from Luke 15:

> Dic mihi, quò tantos properas, puer auree, nummos?
> Quorsum festinæ conglomerantur opes?
>
> Cur tibi tota vagos ructant patrimonia census?
> *Non poterunt siliquæ nempe minoris emi?* (#214)

Crashaw's English version reads as follows:

> Tell me bright Boy, tell me my golden Lad,
> Whither away so frolick? why so glad?
> What all thy Wealth in counsaile? all thy state?
> Are Husks so deare? troth 'tis a mighty rate. (#26)

Knowing the end of the story, Crashaw can neatly join the initial
expectation felt by this "bright Boy" to his later experience, where
he will grovel in a pigsty fighting the swine for their husks to eat.

The remaining characteristics—repetition, juxtaposition, paradox, and pun—are important not only because each defines a
particular rhetorical technique but also because, in the hands of
Crashaw, each enables a reader to perceive a truth that might
otherwise go unnoticed. Repetition is often used for emphasis, as in
an epigram on Mary and Joseph being turned away at the inn

("Non erat iis in diversorio locus"); the poem, though, keys not to
the rejection of *them* ("iis") but to the more profound rejection of
Him ("Illi"):

> Illi non locus est? Illum ergò pellitis? Illum?
> Ille *Deus*, quem sic pellitis; ille *Deus*.
>
> O furor! humani miracula sæva furoris!
> Illi non locus est, *quo sine nec locus est*. (#94)

> (There is no place for Him? Therefore you drive Him away?
> Him? He is God, whom thus you drive away. He is God.
>
> Oh madness! cruel wonder of human madness!
> There is no place for Him without whom there is no place at all.)

The importance of the person not yet born and the speaker's
amazement at the action are underscored through the repetition of
the pronoun ("Illi . . . Illum . . . Illum . . . Illi") and the repeated
identification of who He is: "Ille Deus." Repetition is also used to
point out the theme and, frequently, the paradox of a situation. A
man afflicted with dropsy is said repeatedly to have developed a
new thirst ("sitis"); being cured of his thirstiness *by* Christ has given
him a new thirst *for* Christ (#209). The ungrateful lepers ("Leprosi
ingrati") who are healed by Christ and then leave him are accused
of thus acquiring a new disease: healing became itself a disease
("Ipsa etiam morbus sic *medicina* fuit")(#217). Because Christ
brought him peace ("pacem"), the poet prepares himself for war
("bella"), but the war he must fight is a spiritual war with those who
might threaten his peace (#252).

Repetition also joins with pun, as the poet plays on and works
through a word or phrase to get to the various meanings and the
hidden truth it possesses. Christ's rejection by his own people
("consanguinei" or blood-relation) leads the poet to observe
sarcastically that the thief on the cross was a closer blood-brother
("consanguineus") to Him (#136). Through paradox, pun, and
repetition, Crashaw searches for the meaning behind Saul's
blinding on the road to Tarsus (Acts 9:3):

> Quæ lucis tenebræ? quæ nox est ista diei?
> Nox nova, quam nimii luminis umbra facit!

An Saulus fuerit cæcus, vix dicere possum;
Hoc scio, quòd *captus lumine* Saulus erat. (#304)

(What darkness of light? what night of day is this?
A new night, which the shade of excessive light makes!

Whether Saul was blind I am hardly able to say;
I know this, that Saul was captured by light.)

The epigram effectively progresses from a literal focus to a metaphorical and religious one: the blindness Saul experiences from excessive brightness makes him a captive of the light of Christ.

As we see in this poem, Crashaw sometimes describes an event while joining to it circumstances from a future situation; in this case the impact of Saul's blindness is enhanced by the recognition that he is the Paul who will for the rest of his life be *"captus lumine."* Or, to add insight, Crashaw will juxtapose one biblical event with another, increasing our understanding of each. The people of Herod acclaim him God, but the worms will later claim his flesh in a kind of perverse sacrament (#313). As we saw earlier, Peter's action of cutting off the ear of a foe ironically anticipates his coming denial. The incident of Dives scorning the weeping Lazarus is joined to the recognition that Dives, in hell, will soon have greater cause for weeping (#215). The Latin epigram on Luke 11:27, like its more famous English counterpart ("Blessed be the paps"), portrays the infant Jesus gaining nourishment by sucking from the breast; he, in turn, becomes the source of nourishment through His death (#165).

The verbal pun is a kind of concentrated juxtaposition, a way of providing rhetorical pleasure while signifying two senses of a word simultaneously, thereby, as with larger instances of juxtaposition, allowing a reader to see more profoundly into the truths of his subjects. The infant martyrs, we are told, will no longer receive their mothers' milk; they will encounter a new "milky way" (*"lactea . . . via"*) in their heavenly home (#112). The jailor guarding the imprisoned Peter is admonished not to worry about bolting the door; the "key" ("clavis") Peter has in opening the doors is that he does not need a key ("clave") (#312). Observing the faith of the Canaanite woman, the poet comments that faith ("fidem") is of the feminine gender in more ways than grammatical (#183).

Crashaw's use of the pun also frequently leads to the most prominent feature of the epigrams, the paradox. Crashaw will play on a word in order to penetrate to the paradox concealed within it:

> Monstrat Joannes Christum. haud res mira videtur:
> Vox unus, verbum scilicet alter erat.

> Christus Joanne est prior. hæc res mira videtur:
> Voce suâ verbum non solet esse prius. (#89)

(John makes Christ known. This fact seems not at all astonishing:/For sure, one was the Voice, the other the Word./Christ exists before John. This fact does seem astonishing:/A word does not usually exist before its voice.)

The poem exhibits several important devices—pun, repetition, juxtaposition—but it seems evident that here, as so frequently, Crashaw's ultimate goal is to reveal the paradox implicit in the titles given to John and Christ.

Paradox is pervasive throughout the epigrams, both as technique and as the controlling vision of poems as a whole. Words, situations, and actions all point finally to the surprising revelation, the mystery, the apparent untruth shown nonetheless to be true. The man at the pool of Bethesda (John 5) who, because of his disease, is healed by Jesus, is judged by the poet to have been fortunate in that he has been miserable. His disease-ridden life now healed by Jesus is described oxymoronically as a fortunate shipwreck ("naufragium felix"), a healing storm ("medicæque procellæ"), and, finally, a precious calamity ("tempestas . . . pretiosa")(#149). The faith of Thomas, which demands that he be allowed to touch the wounds of Christ, is a cruel faith ("sæva fides"). Speaking to Christ in another epigram, the poet acknowledges that Christ's death provides life for him while his own life is death to Christ ("Mors tua vita mihi est; mors tibi, vita mea") (#189). Anyone who does not believe Christ's miracles is said to be himself a miracle (#243). Because Mary was the faithful daughter of God ("Fida Dei . . . filia") she will now be His mother (#92). Jesus, as the leader of His people, must be overthrown in order for the people to have their lives safely secured (#259). The virgin holding the infant Jesus must look down in order to see heaven (#96).

The prominence given to paradox suggests how fully Crashaw sees the principle of the Incarnation residing in other circumstances. If the miracle of the Incarnation is true, then nothing is too farfetched or impossible. The Christian poet who can thus see into the mystery of things and who can communicate that mystery to others follows a high and honored position. Beyond the exercises, beyond the impressive rhetorical flourishes, beyond the wit—this is surely Crashaw's goal in the epigrams. Through wit, surprise, irony, and, especially, through paradox, he presents the vision of a world burdened by misery and sin but given new hope by Christ.

C. Crashaw's Epigrammatic Style

The epigrams stand on their own as an important early achievement in Crashaw's poetic career; furthermore, they serve as a kind of personal apprenticeship for Crashaw, introducing him to techniques, themes, and images that are explored, sometimes with quite different effects, in later poems. We see, for example, Crashaw's occasional preoccupation with images of liquefaction, especially blood and water. On one level these images depend ultimately on the paradoxical conjunction of blood and water at the climactic event of the Incarnation, the crucifixion. In one of his epigrams on the crucifixion, the blood becomes wine which in turn is diluted by the water that also flows at the occasion (#269); in another, the blood from the wounds mixes with the tears from the eyes of the weeping Magdalen (#271). Crashaw also joins the early wounding of Jesus in his circumcision to the later wounding of Jesus on the cross; as in his much later hymn on "New Year's Day," he sees the first event dramatically anticipating the second (#s 101, 103). The tears of the suffering Christ, both before and during the crucifixion, call up imagery of a similar effect (#s 233, 234, 235, 272); in another example, the crown of thorns, like the spear thrust in the side, produces blood that yields life to recipients (#267).

We see, furthermore, several examples of the paradoxical image that, largely because of "The Weeper," has probably become Crashaw's best known: the conjunction of water and flame. One epigram calls attention to two of Christ's miracles: curing a woman with fever and healing a man sick with dropsy (#142). Crashaw, in effect, invents the paradox by bringing together two widely separated biblical passages (Mark 1 and Luke 14) and joining the actions in a unified portrait. Thus, through this imagined reciprocity, the flames ("ignes") of the one miracle are said to be immersed in the waters ("aquas") of the other, but so are those waters vanquished by those flames. Also anticipating the later Crashaw, both in subject and in imagery, is an epigram on the Magdalen washing the feet of Christ with her tears and drying them with her hair:

> Unda sacras sordes lambit placidissima: flavæ
> Lambit & hanc undam lucida flamma comæ.
>
> Illa per has sordes it purior unda; simúlque
> Ille per has lucet purior ignis aquas. (#163)

Crashaw's English version also explores the imagery and paradox to be found in later poems, notably "The Weeper" and the Teresa poems:

> Her eyes flood lickes his feets faire staine,
> Her haires flame lickes up that againe.
> This flame thus quench't hath brighter beames:
> This flood thus stained fairer streames. (#15)

It is, finally, in their consistent assumption of a paradoxical mode and vision that the epigrams as a group point us to the Crashaw of later poems. What we see here in brief we see later with greater expansion. But always, in a sense, Crashaw's poetry is tied to the epigrammatical moment: the sudden revelation, the surprising paradox, the revealed mystery. Crashaw, one reader has acutely observed,

was hardly content with a thought until he had found the angle from which its paradox might be seen; nor was he satisfied with that expression of his thought which did not pack pun and metaphor into an antithetical couplet as neatly as possible. His intellect circled and swooped; it was incapable of direct flight. It was erratic in its aim, but constant in method.[20]

II   *The Early Translations*

It is a vulgar error, in translating poets, to affect being *fidus interpres . . .*

for it is not his business alone to translate language into language, but poesy into poesy; and poesy is of so subtle a spirit, that in pouring out of one language into another, it will all evaporate; and if a new spirit be not added in the transfusion, there will remain nothing but a *caput mortuum*.[21]

These comments from Sir John Denham (1615–1669) indicate both the possible restrictions and the potential freedom for a poet seeking to capture in his native tongue the work of another poet. One inclination is to be *fidus interpres*, to reclaim as literally and systematically as possible the language of the original. And the drive to do more, to capture not just the language but the spirit of the original and to bring to the translation the power of one's own verse, is equally strong, especially for the poet of some accomplishment.

The epigrammatic form posed clear formal restrictions for Crashaw; the translating of someone else's work necessarily invited linguistic and topical restrictions. Both the epigrams and the early translations were valuable poetic exercises for the poet—and a number of selections are more accomplished and more important than that designation might imply—for each encourages creativity within a medium that is either highly structured or partially predetermined. In both forms he succeeded and in both we see the poetic roots of the style which, growing under various influences and through various forms, culminates in the Baroque.

Alexander Grosart was one of the first commentators to single out the translations as worthy of particular praise: "the genius of Crashaw," he observed, "shines with its fullest splendour in his translations, longer and shorter."[22] No doubt Grosart had in mind more poems than those to be considered in this discussion of his early efforts, for the total of Crashaw's poems that are translations, that are in some sense "Englished" out of other languages, is over twenty-five. They range from the four-line brevity of "In amorem divinum" (On Divine Love) from Hermann Hugo's *Pia Desideria* (1624) to Crashaw's expansion of the Jesuit Famianus Strada's Latin version of "Musicks Duell" and to his most sustained effort, his translation of the sixty-six *ottave* of Marino's *Sospetto d'Herode*. Chronologically, they range from such early efforts as his versions of two Psalms (probably pre-1630) through his translation of *Sospetto* (1637) to his paraphrases of some of the great medieval hymns of the church, some of them written during the last four years of his life. And, finally, in fidelity to the original the translations vary from the strict rendering of the Italian song "To thy Lover" or "Out of Grotius his Tragedy of Christes sufferinges" to the free and highly expanded versions of "Musicks Duell" or the later "O Gloriosa Domina."[23]

The Renaissance was an age characterized by adventure and exploration, leading to new discoveries in the physical world and a new learning in the intellectual one. It was, in this spirit, a great age of translation as well.[24] Writers experienced in the schools described at the beginning of this chapter felt no inhibitions in translating, borrowing from, or otherwise using ancient authors, for such an effort was a healthy and vigorous means of bringing humanistic learning more immediately to a native land and language. Just as a Renaissance writer felt few restrictions in borrowing from an original so he also felt less obliged to be mechanically faithful in a translation. Renaissance theories of translation encourage a faithful and rich reproduction of the spirit and pleasure of the original more than a literal rendering. George Chapman, an older contemporary of Crashaw, puts the case for free translation strongly: "[H]ow pedantical and absurd an affectation it is," he says,

in the interpretation of any author . . . to turn him word for word, when (according to Horace and other best lawgivers to translators) it is the part of every knowing and judicial interpreter not to follow the number and order of words but the material things themselves, and sentences to weigh diligently, and to clothe and adorn them with words, and such a style and form of oration, as are most apt for the language into which they are converted.[25]

The best translation, said Dryden later in the century, is that which attempts no exact transcription but a poem that provides its own pleasure, a poem that the original author, "if he were living, and an Englishman . . . wou'd probably have written."[26]

Crashaw's early translations are a mixture of the very literal and the relatively free renderings of Greek, Latin, and Italian originals. As we might expect, several of the earliest translations, the efforts of a poet still feeling his way, are the most exacting in their duplication of the originals, while the later ones, most notably "Musicks Duell" and *Sospetto*, reveal a more confident and more independent approach to the art of translation.

Among Crashaw's earliest poems are his paraphrases of Psalm 23

and Psalm 137. For both Psalms Crashaw turns the meditational
solemnity of the original into a more musical, more rhythmically
engaging song. This quality is especially notable in the version of
Psalm 23 ("The Lord is my shepherd"). Crashaw infuses his own
more exuberant spirit into the original and expands it, as the
opening lines demonstrate: "Happy me! o happy sheepe!/Whom
my God vouchsafes to keepe/Even my God, even he it is,/That
points me to these wayes of blisse." The Authorized Version reads,
"He leadeth mee beside the still waters"; Crashaw turns the "still
waters" into a more active force: "At my feet the blubb'ring
Mountaine/Weeping, melts into A Fountaine,/Whose soft silver-
sweating streames/Make high Noone forget his beames" (13–16).
The six-verse brevity of the original is expanded into a seventy-
two-line song in Crashaw's version—more obviously joyful, musical, and decorative. Expansion and decoration are equally evident
in Crashaw's version of Psalm 137, the lament of the children of
Israel in bondage; he follows the progression of the original quite
closely but expands and embellishes its lean melody. In doing so he
reveals a Spenserian floridity that is transformed into the more
Baroque quality of his later verse.

Among classical and neo-Latin writers, Crashaw composed
translations of poems by Heliodorus, Moscus, Ausonius, Martial,
Petronius, Virgil, and Horace. More sustained efforts among his
earlier pieces are his versions of Grotius's "Tragœdia Christus
Patiens" and his three elegies on "The Complaint of the Forsaken
Wife of Sainte Alexis," translated from the Latin elegies of the
Jesuit François Remond. The first is a fairly strict rendering of
Grotius's portrayal of Christ's lament for His sufferings, and it is
likely an academic exercise.[27] The three elegies on the wife of St.
Alexis are engaging pieces, all presented from the wife's perspective and treating her disappointment when her husband deserted
her on his wedding day in order to commit his life to poverty and
piety. Warren sees the elegies as evidence of Crashaw's interest in
"Catholic themes and attitudes";[28] they are, more obviously, an
indication of his early interest in the qualities of sainthood that play
so vital a role in some later poems.

III   Sospetto d'Herode

Most of the poems mentioned thus far are of limited significance
and influence. Crashaw's most important translation, his version of

Marino's *Sospetto d'Herode* (The Suspicion of Herod), has more far-reaching effects. Crashaw's poem is a translation of Book One of Marino's longer work, *La Strage degl' Innocenti* (The Massacre of the Innocents), first published posthumously in 1632. Crashaw's *Sospetto* was probably translated in 1637 and is thus evidence of a continuing interest in the poet of *la meraviglia*, an interest that began at least as early as the beginning of the decade.[29]

Giambattista Marino was born in Naples in 1569 and died in the same city in 1625. He wrote numerous works, many of them highly regarded in his day and after, and enjoyed a considerable reputation as a poet of conceited and witty verse. His many short lyrics and sonnets were well known and translated by Crashaw and others, and his influence was decisive both in Italy and beyond his homeland. In large measure Marino's contemporary reputation rested on two long works, *L'Adone* and *La Strage*. *L'Adone* is a long and convoluted poem, written over a period of more than thirty years and virtually impossible to classify. Its subject is the myth of Venus and Adonis, but its digressions, autobiographical allusions, and generic disruptions produce a curious but "richly polyphonic composition."[30]

La Strage degl' Innocenti was begun as early as 1605 or 1606, but Marino continued to work on the poem intermittently nearly until his death.[31] The theme of the Massacre of the Innocents was a popular one in the Middle Ages and Renaissance, and Marino's poem only enhanced the contemporary audience's fascination for the subject. In the original publication of the poem *La Strage* was divided into two books of *ottave*, but most subsequent editions are divided into four: *Il Sospetto di Erode* (The Suspicion of Herod—sixty-six *ottave*); *Il Consiglio de'Satrapi* (The Council of Governors—146 *ottave*); *L'Esecuzione della Strage* (The Execution of the Massacre—ninety *ottave*); and *Il Limbo* (Limbo—113 *ottave*). Book One introduces Satan who, pondering his fallen state, seeks revenge against God for casting him off. Spiteful and tormented, he sends Cruelty to Herod to warn him of the birth of a child king who will threaten his reign. Book Two opens with a discussion between Herod and his Council and their subsequent decision to have all young Hebrew children killed and closes with the holy family fleeing into Egypt. Book Three portrays numerous massacre scenes, pathetic and grotesque, "passing before our eyes like the narrative sequences of medieval painting."[32] Book Four answers the slaughter of Book Three with the horror of poetic

justice. Determined that no child of the Hebrews be left alive,
Herod soon finds that his child too is dead. He is condemned by his
wife just before her suicide and is left with grief and pain. The final
ottave portray the spiritual victory that Herod's evil has ironically
produced; the souls of the children fly to Limbo, where they are
met and honored by David.

Parts of *La Strage*, particularly in Book Three, exemplify the
sensuousness and intensity typical of Marino's work as a whole. At
one point, for example, we witness the slaughter of an infant and
the anguish of the mother:

> Tal divenne colei, cosi la punse
> Punta d'acuto duolo, a venne meno,
> Su'l caduto figliuol cadde, e congiunse
> Mano à man, volto à volto, e seno à seno.
> Stillò dal cor licor pietoso, & unse
> Le piaghe acerbe, ond'era sparso, e pieno,
> Sciolse ella gli occhi, egli le vene, e quanto
> Egli di sangue, ella versò di pianto. (III, 24)[33]

An English translation of *La Strage* published in 1675 (by T. R.)
captures the flavor of Marino's spirit and imagery in a version that
is also fairly literal:

> Such she appears, and such the wounds, and pains
> Of her sharp grief, nor is she less distress'd:
> On her faln Son she falls, her hands enchains
> In his; joyns face to face, and breast to breast;
> The piteous humour melts her heart and rains
> Into his wounds, which are, by that oppress'd:
> He bleeds, she weeps, and her sad flux of tears,
> A due proportion with his bleeding bears.[34]

The typical Marinesque metaphor, of which the above passage
may be taken as an example, is highly rhetorical, decorative, and
often repeated. Although not intentionally obtuse or obscure, it
invites surprise or a witty recognition as part of its intended
response. Furthermore, though it does not neglect the intellect, "its
main appeal is . . . to the reader's delight in the witty manner by
which a thing has been made more sensuously vivid."[35] Clearly
certain elements of Marino's style are important in a consideration
of the development of Crashaw's poetic manner—the primacy of
wit, the prominence of decorative images, a variety of figures of

rhetoric, the development of verse marked by sensuousness. But Crashaw's translation of *Sospetto* invites some cautious judgments as well, for in general *La Strage* is an example of a more subdued Marino, and the sensuousness evident in the quoted stanza is, for this poem, less the rule than the exception. Crashaw is thus translating a relatively plain Marino, and we are left to wonder if the more "Marinesque" style of Crashaw's translation (but not, ironically, of the original) does not result from more native influences, both literary and religious, than has been previously supposed. Crashaw could look to Spenser for luxury and sensuousness, to Donne for an ever-present wit. If he looked also to Marino for an enhancement of such qualities, he is not the neophyte that some have thought him to be.

When Crashaw began his translation of *Sospetto* he may have contemplated completing all of *La Strage*, but we have no way of knowing.[36] We do know that, in choosing *Sospetto*, Crashaw chose a poem characterized by a more direct, even "austere" poetic statement.[37] Crashaw's version, although structurally and rhythmically true to the *ottava rima* of the original, is much freer in its emotional qualities, more dependent on connotation, on vivid and rich imagery, on sensuous language. Crashaw's *Sospetto* is an excellent example of a translation that bridges the very literal and the very free; it is between his version of Grotius, for example, and his loose "translation" of "Musicks Duell." Never aiming for a strict rendering, Crashaw nonetheless never departed from the substance of the original, using it and refurbishing it with his distinct style.

The sixty-six *ottave* of *Sospetto* are divided as follows: (1–4) Introduction and invocation, to the Muse and to Antonio, Duke of Alba and Viceroy of Naples;[38] (5–10) Satan is introduced "Below the Botome of the great Abysse," having been thrown down by God; (11–20) The beginning of Satan's ponderings, his anticipation of the circumstances of the birth of "A mighty Babe," and the growth of his "new Rage"; (21–24) Satan attempts to comprehend the central mysteries and paradoxes of faith, but they remain for him "knotty Riddles" that entangle "his lost Thoughts"; (25–32) This ruler of hell, anticipating Milton's Satan, alternately despairs and drives himself still to act;[39] (33–46) Applauded by other occupants of hell, Satan calls on Cruelty to aid him in the vengeance he will seek; (47–59) Cruelty hastens to earth, there to plant suspicion in the mind of the sleeping Herod by appearing as the ghost of his dead brother Joseph and warning him of the "most strange Babe"; (60–64) Herod awakens and reacts with fear and suspicion, intending to meet with his counselors in the morning; (65–66) The poem ends with questions mocking the great king's fear of a lowly babe whose armor is "a few thin clouts," whose army is "rude Shepheards."

Crashaw's more lively and more decorative version of the events is apparent throughout the poem. Marino introduces Satan in a relatively cold and straightforward manner:

> Sotto gli abissi, in mezzo al cor del Mondo
> Nel punto universal de l'universo,
> Dentro la boglia del più cupo fondo
> Stassi l'antico spirito perverso.
> Con mordaci ritorte un groppo immondo
> Lo stringe di cento aspidi à traverso.
> Di tai legami in sempiterno il cinse
> Il gran Campion, che'n Paradiso il vinse.

The 1675 English version remains essentially passive and static in its portrait:

> Under the vast Abyss, near to the Heart
> O'th'Universe, and Center of the World;
> Within the Gulph of the profoundest part
> Stood the old Spirit, which from Heav'n was hurl'd;
> About whose Loyns, with horrid jaws retort,
> Myriads of Aspes in filthy knots are curl'd,
>   Subdu'd in Paradise, with those dire Chains,
>   The Angel bound him to Eternal Pains.

Crashaw increases the energy of the poem through the use of more active verbs and through a more colorful portrait of Satan:

> Below the Botome of the great Abysse,
> There where one Center reconciles all things;
> The worlds profound Heart pants; There placed is
> Mischifes old Master, close about him clings
> A curl'd knot of embracing Snakes, that kisse
> His correspondent cheekes: these loathsome strings
>   Hold the perverse Prince in eternall Ties
>   Fast bound, since first he forfeited the skies. (st. 5)

Marino's "mezzo al cor del Mondo" and T. R.'s "Heart/O'th'Universe, and Center of the World" are stale images of location. Crashaw converts the trite metaphor into a vital image, suggestive of both place and emotion, as "the worlds profound Heart pants." Furthermore, Crashaw creates from the images of torment and captivity the implication of a kind of perverse love relationship, as the "embracing" serpents "kisse" Satan's "correspondent cheekes." Little in Marino's stanza is original or even very imaginative; it is instead largely dependent on familiar and uninspired images. Crashaw works from the conventional verse of Marino to create a more vivid and more compelling art.

The pattern of Crashaw's enhancement of Marino, evident in the stanza on Satan, is representative of the poem as a whole. In stanza 40 Marino's "Vendetta" is sitting on a doorstep brandishing in her hand a naked, blood-stained sword ("e'n mano/Spada brandisce insanguinata ignuda"); Crashaw's image recognizes both the royal purple of the proud goddess and the red of her bloody doings: "There has the purple *Vengeance* a proud seat,/Whose ever-brandisht Sword is sheath'd in blood." The light imagery introduced but not emphasized in Marino's stanza 22 ("Che l'incompreso, & invisibil lume/Si riveli, à Pastor mentre, che nasce") and reflected in T. R.'s close translation ("Th' Incomprehensible, Invisible Light/When born, to Shepherds should revealed be") is heightened and made more fully metaphorical in Crashaw's version: "That the Great Angell-blinding light should shrinke/His blaze, to shine in a poore Shepheards eye."

Crashaw's originality does not usually lie in new or startling images not found in the original; more characteristically, he takes what is stated plainly or tritely in Marino and enhances it, vivifies it, and expands it in his version. We see this effect in the stanzas that must have caught Crashaw's eyes like no others, the recitation of the central paradoxes of the Christian faith, brought so dramatically to attention by having the mighty ruler of Hell contemplate the truths revealed in the birth of a mere babe. Marino planted the seeds of the divine mysteries in his original, but in Crashaw they grow and flourish and dominate our perception of the event and its significance. In stanza 21 Satan tries to understand the mysteries but fails:

> But these vast Mysteries his senses smother,
> And Reason (for what's Faith to him?) devoure.
> How she that is a maid should prove a Mother,
> Yet keepe inviolate her virgin flower;

How Gods eternall Sonne should be mans Brother,
Poseth his proudest Intellectuall power.
How a pure Spirit should incarnate bee,
And life it selfe weare Deaths fraile Livery.

For three stanzas following, Crashaw continues to expound on the "knotty Riddles" that bring hope to humanity but only anguish and frustration to Satan. That fascination for paradox evident in Crashaw's epigrams is thus prominent here as well. Writing his translation in 1637, Crashaw must have felt even more strongly that the meaning of the Incarnation event was paradoxical at its center, and that it provided a vision, as well as a meaning and a device, that he could embrace theologically and poetically.

A Continental influence has always been perceived in Crashaw, and it is surely one of the qualities that give his art a distinct character. Nonetheless, with what we are learning of the sweeping cast of developing styles in the seventeenth century, on the Continent and in England as well, it is no longer convincing to assume such a dominant influence from Marino alone.[40] Crashaw no doubt reflects the influence of Marino, but he was not so dependent on him in the development of his own style as some have assumed. Both English and Continental writers contributed to the creation of Crashaw's highly rhetorical style, the prominence given to metaphor and paradox, the flourish and flair that characterize not just Crashaw's art but so much of that poetry labeled Metaphysical and Baroque. And the influence of the Laudian atmosphere in which he was increasingly engulfed must have been substantial, guiding him toward the heightened sensuousness for which his later verse is noted. James Mirollo, coming at Crashaw from Marino, effectively states the case for Marino's certain but limited influence: "Crashaw was concerned with a minor part of Marino's output, with those elements of his style which are the least original with him; hence the Italian's influence was important but not crucial."[41]

The epigrams and early translations, specifically Sospetto d'Herode, reveal Crashaw's early and ongoing interest in a highly rhetorical and figured style. Working in the compact form of the epigram Crashaw demonstrates the poetic devices of a student who knows his poetry and his rhetoric books well. Sensuousness is diminished, yet plain statement is equally rare; imagery, metaphor, and paradox are rich and varied. The *Sospetto* is the work of a poet still fascinated by many of the same qualities—figures, tropes, and images of a vivid and compelling variety. In the *Sospetto*, as well, we see a desire to embellish, to arouse, or more simply, to delight, through language and imagery that, while not shunning the intellect, has a more overtly sensuous appeal. The epigrams and translations are justly considered part of Crashaw's "apprenticeship," particularly if in so designating them we have in mind the most prominent and most important of his later religious verse. Between the writing of most of the epigrams and the writing of *Sospetto*, however, Crashaw's creativity was engaged by more mundane matters that occupied the attention of a writer of numerous secular and occasional poems. If the sacred muse eventually called him to a style that was richly figured and ornate, the secular muse, as we shall see, ordinarily insisted on more modest achievements in a more subdued style—an elegy for a friend, a poem on the king, a celebration of love.

CHAPTER 3

Delights of the Muses:
The Secular and Occasional Poems

R EADING the whole of *Delights of the Muses*, we are struck
first of all by the variety of the collection—a variety of subject, meter, and form. Crashaw wrote poems on the king's coronation, on his return from Scotland, on his recovery from smallpox,
on the births of princes and princesses, and on the royal family
generally; he wrote numerous elegies on friends, acquaintances,
and, presumably, strangers; although his love poems are few, he
wrote three that tantalize us through their contrasting qualities:
"Wishes. To his (supposed) Mistresse," "Loves Horoscope," and
"Epithalamium." Further, he wrote poems that serve as commentary for book illustrations; translations of over a dozen Latin,
Greek, and Italian verses on such subjects as Nature, classical gods
and goddesses, heroes and ordinary mortals; poems on the gunpowder treason of Guy Fawkes; and poems that serve as witty
moralisms on the conduct of human life. The list is not complete,
but it should demonstrate the breadth of the young Crashaw's
poetical interests and obligations.

In matters of versification, Crashaw shows a marked preference
for the iambic tetrameter and pentameter couplet, a style he can
adapt both to the Metaphysical harshness of lines from "On the
Gunpowder-Treason,"

> Dull, sluggish, He! what more than Lethargy
> Gripes thy cold limbes soe fast, thou canst not fly,
> And start from of thy center? hath heavens love
> Stuft thee soe full with blisse, thou can'st not move? (3-6)

and to the more Spenserian opening of "Upon the birth of the
Princesse Elizabeth,"

> Bright starre of Majesty, oh shedd on mee
> A precious influence, as sweet as thee.
> That with each word, my loaden pen letts fall,
> The fragrant spring may be perfum'd withall. (1–4)

It is this basic pattern that lies behind the musical quality and lyrical grace of "Musicks Duell," a poem whose style is notable not for its variation but for its nearly perfect cohesion of musical subject and lyrical effect. When Crashaw describes the heightened effort of the lutenist we are encouraged to "hear" the rhapsodic sounds he makes:

> The humourous strings expound his learned touch,
> By various Glosses; now they seeme to grutch,
> And murmur in a buzzing dinne, then gingle
> In shrill tongu'd accents: striving to bee single.
> Every smooth turne, every delicious stroake
> Gives life to some new Grace; thus doth h'invoke
> Sweetnesse by all her Names; thus, bravely thus
> (Fraught with a fury so harmonious)
> The Lutes light *Genius* now does proudly rise,
> Heav'd on the surges of swolne Rapsodyes. (127–36)

Two elegies further illustrate Crashaw's attention to sound and rhythm and his skill in making the technical element of his verse coalesce with its meaning. The epitaph on "Mr. Ashton a conformable Citizen" is classical in mode and uncomplicated, and the metrical pattern urges a calm and deliberate reading that reinforces the modest achievements of the subject:

> The modest front of this small floore
> Beleeve mee, Reader can say more
> Then many a braver Marble can;
> *Here lyes a truly honest man.* (1–4)

This response to death emphasizes praise and consolation, and the reassuring rhythmical pattern of the poem helps encourage that quality. "Upon the Death of the most desired Mr. Herrys" is a poem in which Death is challenged, not accepted, and again the versification reinforces tone and subject:

> Death, what dost? ô hold thy Blow,
> What thou dost, thou dost not know.

. . . .
What? thinke we to no other end,
Gracious Heavens do use to send
Earth her best perfection,
But to vanish and be gone? (1-2, 25-28)

The abrupt questions, the speechlike effect promoted by caesura
and enjambment, the harsh and skeptical tone all make acquies-
cence in this death difficult. Thus two poems prompted by a
similar event evoke very different responses, not only because of
what the poet says but because of his virtuosity in saying it.

Other poems reveal marked deviations from the dominant
tetrameter/pentameter couplets of most poems in *Delights.*
"Wishes" is a delightful and graceful poem, in no small part
because of its form and rhythm. The poem is built on rhyming
tercets, with lines two and three in each tercet adding a metrical
foot to the previous line:

> Who ere shee bee,
> That not impossible shee
> That shall command my heart and mee;
>
> Where ere shee lye,
> Lock't up from mortall Eye,
> In shady leaves of Destiny. (1-6)

Mario Praz has praised Crashaw's "masterly" translation of a song
by the Italian Ansaldo Ceba, and of particular note is Crashaw's
allegiance to the rhyme and rhythm of the original:[1]

> (Dispiegate
>   Guance amate
>   Quella porpora acerbetta;
>   Che perdenti
>   Che dolenti
>   Fian le rose in su l'herbetta.)
>
> To thy Lover
> Deere, discover
> That sweet blush of thine that shameth
>   (When those Roses
>   It discloses)
> All the flowers that Nature nameth. (1-6)

The most striking example of metrical innovation is seen in Crashaw's "Epithalamium." The poem consists of twelve twelve-line stanzas with alternating rhyme except for a final two couplets. Line lengths vary from dimeter to pentameter, and the essential originality of the verse form is evident especially in the final two couplets, as here from the first stanza:

> where sister budds yet wanting brothers
> kisse their owne lipps in Lieu of others;
> help me to mourne a matchlesse maydenhead
> that now is dead.

Lines 9 and 10 are both iambic tetrameter lines; line 11, a pentameter line, encourages a reader to anticipate an ultimate line of equal length. Instead each stanza closes abruptly with a short dimeter line to complete the final couplet. Each stanza testifies to the innovative effort of the "Epithalamium." In the final stanza Crashaw joins subject, imagery, and verse in a song that is itself a wish for the songlike quality of the married pair whom he is celebrating:

> May their whole life a sweet song prove
> sett to two well composed parts,
> by musickes noblest master, Love,
> playd on the strings of both their harts;
> whose mutuall sound
> may ever meete
> in a just round,
> not short though sweet;
> Long may heaven listen to the songe,
> and thinke it short though it bee long;
> oh prove't a well sett song indeed, which showes
> sweet'st in the Close.

Crashaw is not the most various of poets in his style, but he is clearly attentive to metrical effects and to the subtle but crucial relationship between style and subject. We need not go beyond the secular poems to realize that significant diversity does exist and that, depending on subject, purpose, or occasion, Crashaw was capable of classical elegance, Metaphysical abruptness, and Baroque luxuriousness. It may be too much to say, with Austin

Warren, that an "essential" in Crashaw was a "fascinated concern for style," but his sensitivity to the impact of form and meter is evident throughout the secular canon.[2]

I *The Royalty Poems*

If the three poems on the gunpowder treason are counted as poems on the royalty, the total of such poetic acknowledgments is sixteen—seven written in English and nine in Latin. By subject they break down as follows: the three on the gunpowder treason; two on King Charles's coronation; eight occasioned by births, recent or imminent, of princes and princesses; and one each on the king's recovery from smallpox, on his return from Scotland in 1633, and on the presentation of a book of poems by a number of Cambridge men to Queen Henrietta Maria.

The three poems on the gunpowder treason are likely among Crashaw's earliest, and they are little more than *juvenilia* of indifferent quality. "Dull, sluggish, Ile!" and "Reach me a quill" are similar in a number of ways: each relies frequently on classical allusions and contexts, each calls attention to the horrendous evil that was attempted (it was a "Monster" and the "very Quintessence of villanie"), and each is bookish and dulls the occasion described with a remote and artificial approach. "Grow plumpe, leane Death" is more successful. Although it is more overtly allegorical, it is more original and, in its impact, a more compelling reaction to the threatening plot. Death, "grimme destruction," "lurking trea-son," "palefac't feare" and other "hellish deities" are seen prepar-ing for a meal of King James and his princes. Even such a grisly company cannot feast on that purity; they can only stand and gaze, surfeited "with sweet delight." In a closing of which his father would have been proud, Crashaw determines that only the Pope would have the stomach to devour this "sweet delicious treasury," but that opportunity, of course, is denied him.

The two poems on the king's coronation are quite conventional in theme, imagery, and language, and they may well have been school exercises, for they show Crashaw working through unin-spired allusions and images in his effort to celebrate the occasion of the king's crowning. One poem ("Strange Metamorphosis!") may have been written near the date of the actual coronation, February 2, 1626, but if so Crashaw was only about fourteen at the time; the second poem ("Sound forth, cælestiall Organs") was almost certainly written in 1634 or 1635. The writing of the poem some eight or nine years after the ceremony would further suggest that it may have been part of a university assignment.[3] In both poems Crashaw portrays Charles as a "rising sunne" whose glory surpasses all earthly delights. The first poem hints at the recent death of James as a cause for mourning, but the brilliance of the new king ends the mourning, throws the sun into amazement and awe at his rival, and causes the "melancholy clowds" to vanish. In each poem the king is attended by an only slightly less lustrous family—the queen, a "Virgin Phoenix" in the first poem, a Cynthia in the next; and in the second poem the children born thus far, seen as a "constellation," as beams, and as "three great starres." Anticipating the broad praise in other poems on the royal family, Crashaw here takes the remembered occasion of the coronation to portray the family as the hope of England, as "flaming sparkes of Deity" and "perfect Emblemes of Divinity."

The Latin poems on the king's recovery from smallpox, on his return from Scotland, and on the presentation of a book of poems to the queen were all published originally in Cambridge volumes presented to the royal family. The king's face was unmarked after his successful bout against smallpox in 1632, and Crashaw takes this fact as a sign of his power against the disease. In an effective paradox that closes the poem Crashaw notes that the onslaught of the disease proved the king a man, but his unmarked face proves him a god. In "Rex Redux" Crashaw affirms that neither false nor true dangers have prompted the admiring response of the king's subjects at his return; it is simply that Charles has come back, and that is reason enough for triumph ("Et satis est nostri Carolus nunc causa triumphi"). "Serenissimæ Reginæ librum suum commendat Academia" was written on the occasion of the presentation of a Cambridge volume to the queen following the birth of a son, probably either James (October 1633) or Henry (July 1640). The book is seen as having been "fathered" by the child just born.

Among the eight remaining poems on the births of royal children we see Crashaw working through a number of repeated motifs. Each of the offspring is praised as a model of virtue or as superior to competing glories. In several poems Crashaw praises other members of the family as well, not just the child born. And he frequently elevates the Queen to greatest prominence, for she, we are told repeatedly, is the glorious source of the many progeny. The Latin poems on Princess Mary (b. November 4, 1631) and Princess Elizabeth (b. December 28, 1635) allude to the present winter season and argue that each birth has brought on an early spring. The poem on Mary ("In Natales Mariæ Principis") is addressed to Winter, who is urged to cease its fury ("parce furori") and accept the spring of the new birth. In "In Serenissimæ Reginæ partum hyemalem," on Elizabeth, Crashaw wittily expands on the motif of the seasons in a poem partially addressed to the queen. Since she has brought the spring through this birth, her regular teeming, not conventional months, is proclaimed as the arbiter of the year.

There is also an English poem on Elizabeth's birth, as well as two poems on the birth of James, one on Anne (b. March 17, 1637), and one on Henry. A poem on the frequent deliveries of the Queen and hence on the frequent poetic "deliveries" of Cambridge ("In Reginam, Et sibi & Academiæ semper parturientem") was published in the Cambridge volume *Voces Votivæ Ab Academicis Cantabrigiensibus* commemorating the birth of Prince Henry. In the same volume appeared the most impressive of the nativity odes, "To the Queen, Upon her numerous Progenie, A Panegyrick." "A Panegyrick" is an expanded version of a poem originally written after the birth of James and entitled "Upon the Duke of Yorke his Birth A Panegyricke." In the second version the language of the original is largely retained, but important lines are added on the birth of Elizabeth (63–68) and Henry (76–114).

Although prompted by the birth of Henry, the poem is actually praise of all the offspring and, especially, the mother queen. The 168 lines of the poem are organized as follows: lines 1–8 are addressed to Britain, who must now "spread wide" and "make room" for another guest; lines 9–28 celebrate the children together as "mightie Genii," as "glorious ods" (rare persons), and as the greatness of England itself; lines 29–55 remind us of the previous birth of a "princely Boy," James, who is compared to his older brother Prince Charles—James is Charles's "reall shadow," "Thy little self in lesse," the "well-wrought *copie*" of Charles's "fair *principall*"; lines 55–75 are on another pair, Mary and Elizabeth, praised as "Two silken sister-flowers," "one/Seem'd but the others kind reflexion"; lines 76–114 focus more formally on the newborn prince, whose birth proves that the "pretious store" of the queen has not yet been exhausted. Rebellion, Mischief, War, Blood, and Death are urged to be alert and wary; this birth will defeat them:

> Thy Birthday is their Death's Nativitie;
> They've here no other businesse but to die. (113-14)

The greatest praise is reserved for the queen in lines 115-54. She is seen as a "Deity," as one whose "awfull beauties chase/The Day's abashed glories" (123-24). She is a Cynthia all day, a "Mother-Phenix" whose fruitful womb produces more and more phoenixes and the prospect of continuing progeny. The praise of the queen and all of the children is abundant and eloquent, but Crashaw maintains the poetic convention of final modesty by apologizing for the "untun'd string," the "rurall wreath" of his effort. Only if fired by the eyes of the queen herself can it be made an appropriate offering.

II   *The Elegies*

The elegies comprise the largest single generic group among Crashaw's secular poems.[4] The eighteen selections—over one-fifth of the secular canon—are represented by few examples of enduring quality, but as a collection they are significant in confirming the various poetic modes in which Crashaw wrote. Twelve of the poems are in English, six in Latin, and they are conveniently divided into four groups: (1) two poems—"Upon the death of a freind" and "An Epitaph upon a young married couple"—are of uncertain date and each contains a thematic focus controlled by particular characteristics of its subject. The "freind" was a musician, and the elegy thus consistently puns on various musical terms. The young married couple died at the same time and were buried together; thus Crashaw argues that they are realizing a unity after death that befits their union in marriage; (2) four poems were written early, in 1631 or before, and one of these, "An Epitaph Upon Mr. Ashton a conformable Citizen," is one of Crashaw's distinct successes, an admirable example of his achievement in a Renaissance mode; (3) eight—or possibly seven—lyrics were written in 1631 on the death of a single man, William Herrys of Pembroke College.[5] Written in English and Latin, they range from the unaffected simplicity of the text for

Herrys's memorial monument ("Epitaphium in Dominum Herrisium") to the more disturbing and more Metaphysical impact of
"Upon the Death of the most desired Mr. Herrys" and the poem
titled simply "Another"; (4) finally, four poems come from the last
years of Crashaw's association with Pembroke, 1634 and 1635. One
of these, "Death's Lecture," is, as I suggested earlier, the most
Metaphysical in tone and style of any of Crashaw's poems; two
others, the elegies on "a Gentleman" (Mr. Chambers) and Mr.
Porter, indicate, however tentatively, that Crashaw was beginning
to express the more Baroque quality manifested so importantly in
his later verse.

Six poems may be taken as representative of the aims and modes
of Crashaw's elegiac verse: "Upon Mr. Ashton," "Upon the Death
of the most desired Mr. Herrys" and its companion piece,
"Another," the formal epitaph for Herrys ("Epitaphium in Dominum Herrisium"), "Death's Lecture," and "On the death of Dr.
Porter." The six poems also represent the full chronological range
of Crashaw's funeral elegies: "Upon Mr. Ashton" was probably
Crashaw's earliest elegy, perhaps written even before his admission to Pembroke in 1631; "On the death of Dr. Porter" may be his
last elegy, written in 1635.

The elegy on Ashton is calm and deliberate in tone and
effectively focuses on the virtues of the deceased and on the
worthy emulation of those virtues by those still living. The first
twenty-two lines of the poem praise Ashton's life; the next six
describe his peaceful death in terms that evoke consolation but
little lament; and the final eight lines call on the reader to keep the
spirit of Ashton alive through "thy Imitation bright."

Ashton's modesty and moderation are a significant theme in the
poem, and Crashaw underscores his religious position between the
Puritans and the Romans. The poem likely reveals one Laudian
sympathizer writing about another, for Ashton, we are told,
though a Protestant, was not simply antipapist, and he was not
sympathetic with the Puritan effort to disembellish the church
house:

> Hee was a Protestant at home,
> Not onely in despight of *Rome*.
> Hee lov'd his *Father*; yet his zeale
> Tore not off his Mothers veile.
> To th' Church hee did allow her Dresse,
> True Beauty, to true *Holinesse*. (19-24)

Ashton loved peace in life and found peace in death. Crashaw alters the traditional image of life being ended through the forceful, possibly violent, cutting of life's thread and reveals instead a more tranquil release: "Death tore not (therefore) but sans strife/Gently untwin'd his thread of Life" (29–30).[6] With this kind of life and this kind of death the audience should respond with hope and emulation. While Crashaw acknowledges the memorial aim of his verse he argues as well for a more fitting memorial from those still living: "His better Epitaph shall bee,/His Life still kept alive in Thee" (37–38).

Crashaw's elegy on Ashton is not an exceptional poem, but it is a very good one. We sense the very real presence of subject, speaker, and auditory in the verse and a satisfying conjunction of praise, death, and consolation. Praise and consolation are paramount, virtures are reiterated, death is observed but not really regretted. Lament is not present because the quality of this life and death does not call for it.

"Upon the Death of the most desired Mr. Herrys" and "Another" are companion pieces of a sort, both because they were printed consecutively and because they share a tough outlook on death and its meaning. The first poem opens with an apostrophe and challenge to Death: "Death, what dost? ô hold thy Blow,/What thou dost, thou dost not know" (1–2). Death is seen as a cruel adversary throughout the poem, and the tone is one of dismay and disbelief. Crashaw accepts the existence of analogous acts of destruction in Nature—the fresh bud of a rose mercilessly brought down by the south wind, the early morning sunshine clouded over by a "ruddy storme"—but Herrys's superior goodness argues for his greater protection. That, however, is not to be, and the poem ends, as it begins, with a note of doubt and alarm. Neither the poet at the beginning nor Nature at the end can accept that such a terrible thing has happened.

"Another" is more allegorical but approaches the death of Herrys with a similar emphasis on its cruelty and injustice. As with the previous poem, lament and dismay begin and end the memorial, enclosing a recollection of the virtues death will destroy. Here Crashaw argues that the very colleagues of Death—Fates, Sickness, fever, Destruction—would have acted to save the youth if they could. Herrys, of all people, deserved to be spared: "In briefe, if anyone were free,/Hee was that one, and onely he" (53–54). The lament that follows the reality of death is harsh and unconsoled; with his death "our hopes faire harvest spread/In the dust" (56–57). The fundamental lesson learned is that of Job; humankind is "like dust and ashes" (Job 30:19):

> Sad mortality may hide,
> In his ashes all her pride;
> With this inscription o're his head
> *All hope of never dying, here lyes dead.* (59–62)

Crashaw might have gone on to urge a Christian consolation by portraying—as he does, for example, in the epitaph on the young married couple—the joys experienced by the virtuous Herrys in his new life. But in this poem those joys are notably absent. We are left with the chilling fact of death and its inevitability for all.

The memorial epitaph on Herrys is effective for its clarity, control, and balance. The "Epitaphium" moves from a classical orientation to a more overtly Christian perspective without invalidating either focus. The poem is more formal and public than most of Crashaw's elegies and is thus more biographical, calling attention to Herrys's residences and schooling at Essex and Cambridge (Christ College and Pembroke), to his acknowledged talents, and, finally, to the date of his death, October 15, 1631. Crashaw describes Herrys's classical accomplishments in lines that progress as well toward a fuller recognition of his Christian virtues. Herrys, we are told, was honored as a poet, orator, and philosopher, and, above all, as a Christian. Furthermore, Faith, Hope, Charity, and Humility are all superior in him, although sometimes veiled by a greater modesty ("majore modestia") (35–50). His modesty—that glorious and virtuous dissimulation that hides his great talents ("Pulchram . . . & pudicam dissimulationem")—is revealed even in his death, as he allows himself to be contained under such a small head stone. The virtues of the "Epitaphium" reinforce the human traits emphasized in the poem—modesty, grace, integrity. The memorial balances the classical heritage with a Renaissance Christian perspective to create a simple but moving tribute to the dead man.

"Death's Lecture" was written on the death of a Mr. Stanninow (or Stanenough), Fellow of Queens' College, who was buried on March 5, 1635. It is another of the poems notable for their firm and logical progression, and it works with considerable impact to remind the reader of the gruesome reality of death. In this respect it recalls the tone and aim of "Upon the Death of the most desired Mr. Herrys" and "Another," although here the rhetoric points to an even harsher reality. It is, of course, *Death's* lecture, and we should rightly expect that consolation will be lacking. Indeed the entire poem is a kind of generalized lament, not so much for Stanninow as for humankind as a whole.

Death acts as a summoner, calling forth those physical elements of humankind once so prized but now worth nothing. Youth and Beauty are only "sylken flatteryes [that] swell a few fond howres/Into a false æternity" (9–10). Humanity is seen as if through the eyes of the despairing Hamlet, as that "quintessence of dust":

> Come man;
> Hyperbolized NOTHING! know thy span;
> Take thine own measure here: down, down, and bow
> Before thy self in thine idæa; thou
> Huge emptynes! contract thy self; and shrinke
> All thy wild circle to a Point. (10–15)

These lines aptly convey the essential aim of the poem—to shock humankind into recognizing the insignificance of this life ("Thy neighbourhood to NOTHING") and the grim reality of death. Pride, flattery, beauty, and youth in this poem give way to "death-seal'd lippes," the "curtain'd windows" of eyes, the "brave" posture of death. It is, Death tells us, death itself that is the important truth: "All-daring dust and ashes! only you/Of all interpreters read Nature True" (31–32).

Perhaps because this poem is only tangential to the elegiac mode Crashaw took more liberties than he ordinarily did. The speaker is not a friend or acquaintance but Death itself, and the tone is harsh and unrelenting throughout. If, in view of the other elegies, this poem tells only partial truth about death and what follows, it is a compelling truth nonetheless.

To move from "Death's Lecture" to the elegy on Porter is, on one level, to move from Metaphysical skepticism to Baroque sensuousness. In "An Elegie on the death of Dr. Porter" Crashaw relies more fully on the tears of mourning as the means of consolation in and of themselves. The poem includes several elegiac *topoi* familiar in the history of the genre, and in its appeal to Nature to mourn the death it is firmly grounded in the elegiac tradition. The poem is

addressed to the river Cam, who is urged to halt its progress
momentarily to witness the present mourning. Attention is called
to the mourning scene and, much more briefly, the virtues of
Porter. The four lines that hint at his qualities are closed abruptly:
"Enough is said," and the remainder of the poem urges the river to
"be gone,/And murmur forth thy woes to every flower" (20-21).
The flowers will, in turn, be taught to "sing their saddest Dir'ges"
and stones will weep. At the end of its journey to the ocean the river
Cam can then "weep thyselfe into a sea of teares" (38). The poem
ends with the lines, like the river, nearly overflowing with liquidity
and sweetness. A "bright Christall tide," "mines of Nectar," "sweet
fountains," "a lilly path," "rosy mountaines," and "bubling eyes" all
coalesce in a Baroque phantasmagoria:

> A thousand Helicons the Muses send
> In a bright Christall tide, to thee they tend,
> Leaving those mines of Nectar, their sweet fountains,
> They force a lilly path through rosy mountaines.
> Feare not to dy with greife; all bubling eyes
> Are teeming now with store of fresh supplies. (39-44)

III   *The Love Poems*

To describe the three poems to be discussed in this section as
love poems is somewhat misleading, for only one, "Loves Horoscope," is anything like the response of a poetical speaker to his
beloved. Of the other two, "Wishes. To his (supposed) Mistresse"
is a light and fanciful, albeit thoroughly charming, description of a
hypothetical, "supposed" woman. The "Epithalamium" is an
impressive celebration of love rites, probably those of Sir John
Branston and Alice Abdy in 1635.

"Wishes" is the final poem in the 1646 edition of *Delights* and is
worthy of that ultimate position. It is Crashaw's finest poem in a
Jonsonian mode—simple, restrained, and melodious. The poem
has three divisions: lines 1-15 introduce the aim of the poem and
the subject for whom the wishes are intended; lines 16-105 are
the wishes themselves; lines 106-26 hypothesize that a real person
might fit the role of that "not impossible she"; if there is such a
person, she is urged to enjoy the implicit praise given her in the
poem.

The mistress is "supposed" because no real lady is intended. She is, to be sure, "not impossible," but is essentially a thought, an ideal, a Platonic "Divine *Idæa*" not yet occupying "a shrine/Of Chrystall flesh, through which to shine" (11–12). The wishes themselves are many and encompassing. Eyes, hair, heart, smiles, blushes, joys, days, nights, and hours are all described with near perfection and desired for the lady in that degree. The wishes are intended for a natural beauty, one not dependent on gaudy attire, or rouge, or lipstick to give only a surface attractiveness. She will be modest, charming, and joyful, little possessed of fears or tears, and continually blessed by fulfilling days and nights. Because her beauty and virtue are both natural and profound, she is her own best measure of worth, and the ultimate wish is that she will be so worthy that she will not have need of wishes:

> In her whole frame,
> Have Nature all the Name,
> Art and ornament the shame.
>
> Her flattery,
> Picture and Poesy,
> Her counsell her owne vertue bee.
>
> I wish, her store
> Of worth, may leave her poore
> Of wishes; And I wish—No more. (97–105)

Joseph Summers observes that the poem reveals Crashaw's "tendency toward copious, almost infinite, variations."[7] If so, the variations are of a far different order from those of, say, "The Weeper." Here imagery is subdued, the tone is controlled and witty, and we realize that Crashaw is in perfect command of each new variation. His fancy is apparently given free reign, but he exercises a subtle but firm control as well.

"Loves Horoscope" recalls some of Donne's love lyrics, both in its title and in its tight logical structure. Like Donne, Crashaw adapts astronomical imagery to an earthly purpose, leading to an effective concluding paradox describing the love of the speaker for his "Beauty." The poem entertains the possibility of two external influences on the speaker and his love: the influence of planetary bodies in their spheres, an influence that is denied, and the influence of the Beauty herself, an influence that is confirmed.

The poem develops through three pairs of related stanzas, each pair advancing the analogy between planetary influences and the influence of the Beauty and demonstrating the superiority of her life-giving power. In the first stanza the Heart, the "Mother" of the newly realized Love, inquires among the "conscious Spheares" to determine what omens attended the birth of Love:

> Shee askes if sad, or saving powers,
> Gave Omen to his infant howers,
> Shee asks each starre that then stood by,
> If poore Love shall live or dy. (5-8)

The second stanza redirects the inquiry, however, for the answer to the question of Love's longevity is not to be found among the "conscious Spheares" but through the "new Astrology" learned from the "Face in whose each looke,/Beauty layes ope loves Fortune-booke (11-12). The second stanza thus confirms the significance of her "faire revolutions" that guide the course of Love and determine its fate:

> 'Tis in the mercy of her eye,
> If poore Love shall live or dye. (19-20)

In parallel middle stanzas Crashaw argues that her "milder influence" is great enough to overcome any competing influence from the heavens. In stanza three the heavens are seen as working to provide a happy life for Love by revealing their "best Aspects, twin'd upon/The kindest Constellation" (25-26) and by paving Love's "pathes with all the good/That warmes the Bed of youth and blood" (29-30). These favorable signs are for nought, however, if her eyes "bid Love be gone": "Love ha's no plea against her eye/Beauty frownes, and Love must dye" (31-32). Stanza four reverses the effects. Now the poet imagines that "heavens inauspicious eye/Lay blacke on loves Nativitye" (35-36), that the former "best Aspects" have changed to a "frowne." But if she seeks to "guild the hopes of humble Love" (34), her favorable aspect will overcome heaven's disapproval: "Her Eye a strong appeale can give,/Beauty smiles and love shall live" (39-40).

The final two stanzas are tightly matched sestets and are mutually reinforcing structurally, rhetorically, and thematically. If Love is to live, the poet says in stanza five, it must dwell in her eye, or ear, or breast, or breath. For his Love to live without her is death to Love: "For in the life ought else can give,/Love shall dye although he live" (45–46). If Love is to die, the final stanza proclaims, it will die in her eye, or ear, or breast, or breath. And if Love dies in *her*, it will find life: "While Love shall thus entombed lye,/Love shall live, although he dye" (51–52).

"Loves Horoscope" will come as a surprise to readers who might have been lulled by the relative simplicity and conventionality of many of the secular poems. It is a demanding poem, rigorous in its attention to imagery and idea, and impressive in its steady logical movement to the consummate paradoxes in praise of the Beauty.

Crashaw's "Epithalamium" is a ritual celebration of marriage, beginning before the fulfillment of love and continuing through the marriage event to the prospect of a joyful union and future progeny.[8] The poem opens by focusing on the bride, viewing her virginity, her maidenhead, as the proverbial phoenix seeking to avoid the arrows of Love. Through the first three stanzas the phoenix-maidenhead resists Love out of pride: she is a "fine thin negative thing" pruning "her plumes in selfe loves glasse"; she is a "froward flower" with "peevish pride" and a "foole" with "froward pride." Her resistance is against the natural order, for it freezes "the fruite of faire desire." The phoenix then seeks safety from Love by residing in the bosom of the young woman Alice Abdy (stanza 4), but the safety is shortlived. Love conspires with Branston, and from the "fort" of his eyes arrows are shot that defy resistance (stanza 5).

Stanzas 6 through 9 describe the consummation of love, first by having the phoenix-maidenhead die through the action of Love and then by portraying the more immediate and more human responses of the couple. The phoenix of the poem dies in the flames of Love's making, on "her funerall pyle/the marriage bedd" (65–66). In more human terms the realization of love follows the doubts, uncertainties, smiles, and fears of the new lovers: the "many pretty peevish tryalls/of angry yeelding, faint denyings/melting No's, and milde denyalls/dying lives, and short lived dyings" (73–76). Attention turns more certainly to the "Blessed Bridegroome" in stanzas 8 and 9, as he is the recipient of love and joy from the bride. He receives, but she has more to give: "thrice happy he/partakes her store,/thrice happy she/hath still the more" (89–92). The final three stanzas focus appropriately on the bride

and bridegroom together. He is the "faire oake" to her "Vine," and
their embrace will be mutually fulfilling:

> safe may she rest
> her laden boughes,
> on thy firme breast,
> and fill thy vowes,
> up to the brimm, till she make even
> their full topps with the faire eyed heaven. (113–18)

He will find no charms but from her eyes, she no joy but in his arms.
Their life together is seen in the final stanza as a "sweet song" of
"two well composed parts," a song that, at its end, will be "sweet'st
in the Close."

The "Epithalamium" exhibits an effective harmony of parts—
opening with attention to the bride, then focusing on the groom,
and finally viewing the two together from the perspective of an
outside party. The phoenix image appropriately gives way to more
engaging human acts and feelings. The strands of the poem are
neatly woven throughout, and the verse thus embodies the unity
and concord evident in the couple it celebrates.

IV   "*Musicks Duell*"

"Musicks Duell" is the best known of Crashaw's secular works
and the most frequently praised. It has been called the "secular
triumph of the Crashavian style, and . . . , of its kind, the most
impressive achievement in English poetry."[9] It is one of the few
secular poems that confirm Crashaw's association with the Baroque and has been termed therefore "the height of the baroque
style in English poetry," a poem where "the most profuse luxury is
formed with the most perfect art."[10]

"Musicks Duell" is a free translation of, and a substantial
addition to, the Latin text in the *Prolusiones* of the Jesuit Famianus
Strada, published in 1617. Strada's poem on the musical battle
between a lute-player and a nightingale revived interest in a
traditional subject dating back to the Middle Ages; it prompted
several translations, including poems by John Ford, William
Strode, and others of Crashaw's contemporaries, but Crashaw's is
the most original and most distinguished of the group. The
originality is suggested by the lengths of the Strada poem and

"Musicks Duell." Crashaw takes Strada's fifty-two-line effort and builds it into a 168-line Baroque showplace, over three times the length of the original. The most pronounced addition is in that section of the poem in which Crashaw describes, with increasing emotion and luxury, the final effort of the lutenist to achieve the "*Empyræum* of pure Harmony" to defeat his winged rival. The final sixty-four lines are based on only eighteen lines in the Latin, and the Strada piece contains little of the detail and even less of the grandeur of its translation.

One of the most striking features of "Musicks Duell" is its musical quality, or, more accurately, "its endeavor to produce an emotional effect equal to that . . . gained from music."[11] This is evident not so much in terminology, although the language of music is prominent in the poem, or in the onomatopoetic quality of individual words, although this characteristic too is present, as in the more encompassing musical effect of the rhythm and sound of the poem. The lines on the lutenist's final effort encourage, in their reading, a recognition of the variety and harmony of his notes:

> From this to that, from that to this hee flyes
> Feels Musicks pulse in all her Arteryes,
> Caught in a net which there *Appollo* spreads,
> His fingers struggle with the vocall threads,
> Following those little rills, hee sinkes into
> A Sea of *Helicon*, (119-24)

and later:

> The Lutes light *Genius* now does proudly rise,
> Heav'd on the surges of swolne Rapsodyes.
> Whose flourish (Meteor-like) doth curle the aire
> With flash of high-borne fancyes: here and there
> Dancing in lofty measures, and anon
> Creeps on the soft touch of a tender tone:
> Whose trembling murmurs melting in wild aires
> Runs to and fro, complaining his sweet cares
> Because those pretious mysteryes that dwell,
> In musick's ravish't soule hee dare not tell,
> But whisper to the world. (135-45)

The poem develops a number of contrasts, and its structure encourages us immediately to focus on them. The opening lines

(1–6) set the scene as evening, with the lutenist playing his "gentle aires" in the shade of an oak tree. Nearby is a nightingale (7–14) who hears the song of the lute and strives to "mold the same/In her owne murmures." The man perceives his rival, and "the fight" begins. He plays briefly (15–21); she responds briefly (22–26). His next effort (27–33) begins to take advantage of his more varied instrument, as he gives each string a "capring cheerefullnesse," plays "negligently rash," and finally "Blends all together." The bird "Meets art with art" (34–43) and sings her "cleare unwrinckled song" with accents, diminutives, and warbles. The lute player, amazed, "Straines higher yet" (43–56), and his finger acts as "Moderatour" between "grumbling Base" and the "Trebles Grace," closing "the sweet quarrell" of varying sounds. The nightingale confidently answers him back and, in fact, changes the direction of the challenge. She now sings at length (56–104) and will force the lutenist to answer. She performs her "Sharpe Aires," "thundring volleyes," and "panting murmurs" as if they are pouring out of her "delicious soule" "in streames of liquid Melodie." She sings as a "holy quire," and then triumphantly bursts forth with even more: "Shee opes the floodgate, and lets loose a Tide/Of streaming sweetnesse, which in state doth ride/On the wav'd backe of every swelling straine,/Rising and falling in a pompous traine" (93–96). Finally, she moderates her enthusiasm with the "cool Epode of a graver Noat." As a consequence of all of this, "Her little soule is ravisht" and she is beyond herself as "Musicks *Enthusiast*" (102–104).

The lutenist is angry and ashamed and vows to play to his lute's or the nightingale's defeat. He moves through varying sounds and paces, "The humourous strings expound his learned touch,/By various Glosses; now they seeme to grutch,/And murmur in a buzzing dinne, then gingle/In shrill tongu'd accents: striving to bee single" (127–30). This "fury so harmonious" heaves "on the surges of swolne Rapsodyes." The playing produces a near ecstasy, as if the notes "meant to carry/Their Masters blest soule . . . through all the sphæares/Of Musicks heaven" (146–49). Finally, through all the diversity and strife of sound, "A full-mouth'd *Diapason* swallowes all" (156). The nightingale tries a final time to match the "wild diversities" with the "small size of one/Poore simple voyce, rais'd in a Naturall Tone" (163–64), but it is hopeless. She fails, grieves, and dies, falling on the lute: "o fit to have/(That liv'd so sweetly) dead, so sweet a Grave!" (167–68).

The conflict in the poem is, on one level, between Nature and

Art, the natural song of the bird and the created sound of the man playing on an instrument. It is also a conflict between melody and harmony: the bird can sing only one note at a time; the lute player can mix and blend his "wild diversities" through the power of his fingers. Crashaw implies at the end of the poem, and elsewhere as well, that the nightingale's inability to match the variety and virtuosity of the lutenist is what leads to her defeat and death. William Madsen argues convincingly that the poem communicates on another, more theological level; it advances a conflict, not only of Nature and Art but also of Nature and Grace.[12] Read anagogically the poem suggests the limitations of Nature and the ascendancy of Grace. Nature in the form of the nightingale is restricted to earth; her near ecstasy is not finally to be accomplished. The harmony and rhapsody of the lute suggests, typologically, the order of grace and the achievement of both a musical *Empyræum* and an eternal heaven.

V   *Additional Poems*

Among the remaining secular poems a few merit brief commentary. Two poems were written to accompany engravings in published books. "Upon Bishop Andrewes his Picture before his Sermons" was printed under an engraving of Lancelot Andrewes included in the volume of his *XCVI Sermons* reissued in 1632. The poem is less significant for its quality than for its indication of Crashaw's early reputation and his apparent Laudian sympathies. Laud himself was partially responsible for the publication of the sermons, and it is a notable tribute to Crashaw that he was selected to write the poem for the occasion. Henry Isaacson, a student and later a close friend of Andrewes, wrote a biography of Andrewes and a chronology of kings and monarchs in the world. For the chronology Crashaw wrote a poem describing and interpreting the frontispiece, the poem with the unassuming title, "On the Frontispiece of Isaacsons Chronologie explained." Both poems confirm Crashaw's stature as a youthful but accomplished poet.

"Upon two greene Apricockes sent to Cowley by Sir Crashaw" is a tribute to the poet's friend who was himself a poet. Abraham Cowley's first volume of poems was published in 1633, when he was only fifteen; a second volume followed in 1636, a third in 1637. In that same year Cowley went to Cambridge where he struck up a friendship with Crashaw that was renewed when both of them went to Paris in the mid-1640s. In the poem Crashaw mocks his own poetic gift of "two greene Apricockes" in contrast to the mature fruit of Cowley, who was six or seven years his junior. "How then must these,/Poore fruites," he says, "looke pale at thy Hesperides!" (29–30). Cowley is abundantly praised throughout as the "Young master of the worlds maturitie," and the poem closes "with lines of elegance and power that go quite beyond conventional compliment":[13] "Take them [the poems], and me in them acknowledging,/How much my summer waites upon thy spring."

"To the Morning. Satisfaction for sleepe" is another poem in which Crashaw derides himself, but here the failure is not a tardy poetic genius but a more mundane act: he fell asleep in chapel. The subtitle of the poem in a manuscript, "To the Deane on occasion of sleeping [in] chappell," indicates both the earlier mistake and the source of the poet's present apprehension.[14] Crashaw voices regret at his action and at the unyielding response his lapse provokes. He is downstruck, without "humble fancy" or "nimble rapture": "All these delicious hopes are buried,/In the deepe wrinckles of his angry brow,/Where mercy cannot find them" (30–32). Pledging no more to be the "votery" of the God of Sleep, Crashaw urges Somnus to go where sleep would be more appreciated, among the sorrowful or the sick, "whose pale lidds ne're know/Thy downy finger, dwell upon their Eyes,/Shut in their Teares; Shut out their miseryes" (56–58).[15]

"Temperance. Or the Cheap Physitian Upon the Translation of Lessius" is a testimony to moderation as a key to health and to the necessary alliance of a healthy body and a healthy soul. Leonard Lessius was a Jesuit theologian who published a volume on temperance and health. An English translation of the book, *Hygiasticon: Or the Right course of preserving Life and Health unto extream old Age*, went through two editions in 1634, a third in 1636. Crashaw wrote a shorter poem for the second edition—"To the Reader, upon this Books intent." That poem was combined, with little change, with another poem, "On taking Physicke," to make the poem "Temperance." In fact, the larger poem remains divided into two parts, corresponding to the two original poems. The poet first derides the practice of looking only to the physician for health. The "daring drugg," the "big-nam'd composition," "Th'Oraculous DOCTOR'S mystick bills," or "Certain hard WORDS made into pills" do not guarantee health; what they do guarantee is a "costlyer disease." The key to health, evident in the second half of the poem, is the successful harmony of soul and body, thus confirming "Nature [as] her own physitian." The "well-cloth'd soul" leads not only to health for the young but also to continuing vitality for the old: "a man that can/Live to be old, and still a man" (43–44). Even in death the "soul and body part like freinds" (48). Crashaw ends the poem by urging the reader's application of these suggestions for good health: "This rare one, reader, wouldst thou see?/Hark hither; and thyself be HE" (51–52).

One final poem, the Latin "Bulla," is perhaps the most distinct of any of the poems discussed in this chapter; it is, for certain, quite unlike anything else Crashaw wrote. The subject is a water bubble ("bulla") and the poem is as light and fanciful as the title suggests. We see the bubble in its multi-colored splendor and its light and variegated movement. The bubble then becomes a symbol of all things fleeting or uncertain—the wind, the pride in trinkets, the fragile faith in fortune. The penultimate section of the poem, spoken as if by the bubble, reveals its charm, inconstancy, and beauty, but reminds us, finally, that it is nothing ("O sum, [scilicet, O nihil.]"). In a semblance of an apology, the poet admits at the end that this poetic "bubble" may have gone on too long (through 151 lines). But he wittily reminds the readers that it is only through their reading that the bubble continues to survive; to make it end, lift up your eyes ("Tolle tuos oculos").

This poetic example of Crashaw's "dizzy imagination" provides something of an ironic close to the discussion of the secular poems.[16] Generally, the secular verse reveals a Crashaw who is more subdued, more controlled in his poetic idiom. In the sacred poems we often see Crashaw climbing poetic mountains, more enraptured, more daring, more apt to succeed impressively or fail notably. In the secular poems he remains on level ground, working largely through traditional forms and familiar motifs to make his increasingly mature poetry his own.

CHAPTER 4

Steps to the Temple:
The Sacred Poems

THE 1646 volume of *Steps to the Temple* first brought to the public's eye many of the poems for which Crashaw attained a continuing reputation as, in Abraham Cowley's elegiac description, "poet and saint."[1] The 1648 volume of *Steps*, in addition to presenting revised versions of a number of poems, introduces some important new ones as well, including "Charitas Nimia," "To the Same Party [Mrs. M.R.] Councel concerning her Choise," "The Office of the Holy Crosse" ("Upon our B. Saviours Passion"), the Hymn to the Name of Jesus, the Hymn in the Glorious Epiphanie, the six translations of medieval hymns, and two of the poems inspired by St. Teresa, "The Flaming Heart" and "A Song." The 1652 volume, *Carmen Deo Nostro*, is a more select collection; as the title suggests, it includes no poems that are overtly secular and only four that had been previously grouped within the 1648 *Delights of the Muses*: the elegies on St. Alexis, "An epitaph upon a young married couple," "Death's Lecture," and "Temperance" ("In praise of Lessius"). The volume begins with the only new poem, the tribute "To the Noblest and best of Ladyes, the Countesse of Denbigh," in which Crashaw urges the woman to yield to the Roman communion of which he is now a part, and continues through poems on Christ, poems on the church or its worship, poems on the saints, and, finally, and somewhat anticlimactically, miscellaneous poems on various subjects.[2] That this is the final volume to come directly out of his lifetime provides further evidence that the poet was, during the last years of his writing, turning entirely to religious subjects. The existence of both the religious poems and the secular poems in the volumes of 1646 and 1648 is recognition that the poet there presented could be remembered and honored for both achievements. The final volume suggests that, either to Car or to Crashaw or to both, the poet will be honored solely for his "carmen Deo nostro."

The writer of the Preface to the 1646 and 1648 volumes, although recognizing both sacred and secular verse, does not give anything like equal attention to the *Steps* and the *Delights*. His long and laudatory comments on the divine poems are inadequately matched by his one-sentence tribute to the secular poems: "And those other of his pieces intituled, *The Delights of the Muses*, (though of a more humane mixture) are as sweet as they are innocent."[3] In general the writer points to qualities in the sacred poetry and to accomplishments of the "Divine Poet" that encourage a view of the volume as a product of a rare, and perhaps rarefied, individual. More than merely conventional or exaggerated praise, the Preface isolates the almost unearthly quality of the poetry. The poems will, we are told, "lift thee Reader, some yards above the ground . . . So maist thou take a Poem hence, and tune thy soule by it, into a heavenly pitch; and thus refined and borne up upon the wings of meditation, in these Poems thou maist talke freely of God, and of that other state." Praising Crashaw as "*Herbert's* second," the writer goes on to suggest, at least implicitly, the qualities of *Steps to the Temple* that separate Crashaw's verse from most of Herbert's in *The Temple*. "*Divine Poetry*," he urges, is "the Language of the Angels; it is the Quintessence of Phantasie and discourse center'd in Heaven; 'tis the very Outgoings of the soule; 'tis what alone our Author is able to tell you, and that in his owne verse."

This early commentator and probable friend implies an attitude toward Crashaw's sacred verse that has often been echoed in more recent criticism, that his is a poetry frequently detached from and hovering beyond the plane of ordinary human activity, or even of conventional religious activity, that he, as a poet, had "difficulty in touching earth."[4] This quality is most apparent in those poems in which the influences of the Baroque and the mystical traditions align to produce a verse that exults in its own splendor, in its sensuous and religious ecstasy, in its drive to break the bonds of human restrictions. This ultimate expression of the Baroque is most pronounced in the poems that reflect the influence of St. Teresa and the mystical tradition. In spite of its partial truth, however, the

Preface is also misleading, for a number of poems in *Steps* are more firmly controlled, more earthbound than we might otherwise be led to expect.

I *Herbert's Second*

Although the title of *Steps to the Temple* confirms its association with Herbert's *The Temple*, there is little evidence among the poems as a whole that Crashaw was particularly indebted to Herbert. While Crashaw undoubtedly knew and admired Herbert's verse, and while both were associated with the community at Little Gidding, Crashaw's life and poetry took him beyond the more limited poetic and geographical confines of the Anglican preacher. In two of Crashaw's poems, however, the qualities of Herbert's verse, if not his direct influence, are readily apparent.[5]

"Charitas Nimia. Or the Dear Bargain" and "Office of the Holy Crosse" are in some ways quite unlike each other. The first is a more personal address to God, consisting primarily of questions that imply humankind's uselessness to the Almighty; the "Office," especially in the 1652 expanded version, is a very formal and ritualistic poem presenting devotions for each of the seven prescribed hours of the day. If it was not actually used for devotional purposes, it could have been. Nonetheless, in tone, in simplicity of structure, and, occasionally, even in imagery and diction, both poems are reminiscent of Herbert and suggest that at least here Crashaw may rightly be called "Herbert's second."

"Charitas Nimia" consists of thirteen uneven stanzas dominated by questions posed by the speaker to God, followed by a final two couplets that plead for understanding and renewal. The theme is one found frequently in Herbert and occasionally in Donne: the insignificance of humankind in view of the majesty and goodness of God. The more immediate source is Psalm 144:3–4, notably the Prayer Book version: "Lord, what is man, that thou hast such respect unto him: or the son of man, that thou so regardest him? Man is like a thing of nought: his time passeth away like a shadow."

In tone and focus the poem has two major divisions: the first part (1–28) considers the relationship between God and the whole of "Mankind," and we are only barely aware of a personal voice behind the questions. In the second part of the poem (29–62) and into the resolution (63–66), the speaker's questions become more intense and much more personal; it is no longer "Mankind," but "I" who may be a victim of "mine own madnesses," or "lost in misery," or possessed of a "faithlesse soul." In the resolution the subjective tone continues, as the poet prays for the ability to "see/How dearly thou hast payd for me."

The opening two stanzas of the poem introduce the commercial imagery that is identified in the full title but is not otherwise much explored in the poem:

> Lord, what is man? why should he coste thee
> So dear? what had his ruin lost thee?
> Lord what is man? that thou hast overbought
>   So much a thing of nought?
>
> Love is too kind, I see; and can
> Make but a simple merchant man.
> 'Twas for such sorry merchandise
> Bold Painters have putt out his Eyes. (1–8)

The "sacrifice" of secular Love (Cupid) in being blinded by "Bold Painters" hints at the much greater cost, the "dear bargain," that sacred Love has assumed for humankind, who is no more than "sorry merchandise," "a thing of nought."

From the introduction of this essential mystery, the poet proceeds to elaborate on man's inconsequential position before God: "Alas, sweet lord, what wer't to thee/If there were no such wormes as we?" (9–10). Heaven would still be heaven regardless of the state of humanity, and created things would still adore their creator: the angelic host would sing and praise, the "spheares [would not] let fall their faithfull rounds" (18).

The indictment of humankind continues and becomes more emphatic in the second part of the poem, and the imagery becomes even more debasing. There, beginning in stanza seven (line 29), the poet turns from generalized humanity to himself and his own sins. Only two of the remaining stanzas (eight and nine) denounce human frailty in language that is not accompanied by the intensely personal pronoun. In those two stanzas man is the "desperate Fool," the "worm," the "wanton," "foolish fly." A reading of the lines is, however, strongly affected by the personal note first struck in the final lines of the preceding stanza: "Why shouldst thou bow thy awfull Brest to see/What mine own madnesses have done with me?" (33-34). The decisive change of focus, first indicated in these lines, from generalized humanity to the speaker himself, influences a more intimate reading of the lines immediately following. While all of humanity may be captured in the "desperate Fool," or the "worm" or the "foolish fly," the descriptions carry a more intense, if implicit, self-indictment than do earlier condemnations of insignificant mortals.

The remaining stanzas are entirely personal and the tone and imagery reveal further changes in the aim of the lines. In the first part of the poem the speaker portrays a God who might have remained aloof and majesterial, unaffected and undemeaned by the self-initiated misery of humankind. The final stanzas of the poem, still characterized by questions and by a sense of wonder and awe, reveal that the God who might have remained aloof did not, and that the "dear bargain" has, in all its mystery, been paid. Earlier stanzas seem to be directed to God the Father, who could have continued to receive praise and adoration while ignoring humankind; later stanzas reveal that God the Son, the "Lamb," has already paid the price that so fills the speaker with amazement: "What did the Lamb, that he should dy?/What did the lamb, that he should need,/When the wolf sins, himself to bleed?" (52-54). More personally, the poet is in awe that "the white/Lamb's bosom" must "write/The purple name/Of my sin's shame" (57-60). The resolution of the poem is an effectively brief and controlled statement of the speaker's recognition of the "dear bargain" and of the response demanded of him:

> O my SAVIOUR, make me see
> How dearly thou hast payd for me;
>
> That lost again my LIFE may prove
> As then in DEATH, so now in love. (63-66)

In "Charitas Nimia" Crashaw leads the reader from a generalized view of the condition of "Mankind" to a more private revelation of his own faults and needs. The poem, like many of Herbert's, leads steadily through questions and statements to a conclusion that, although brief, has the impact of a decisive resolution.

"Charitas Nimia" moves from a public mode to a private one; "Office of the Holy Crosse" is both public and private, reflecting both the formal and impersonal character of the liturgy of the church and the more private mode of the Primers from which the poem is derived. In 1648 the hymns for each of the seven devotional hours were printed, followed by an Antiphona, a Recommendation, a Prayer, and a three-stanza poem titled "Christs victory." The hymns in 1648 are headed "Upon our B. Saviours Passion." The 1652 version is expanded into a complete ritual for each hour, consisting, in order, of Versicle, Responsory, Hymn, Antiphona, Versicle, Responsory, and Prayer, and followed, after the final hour (Compline), by "The Recommendation."

The parts of the "Office" relevant to Crashaw's poetry are the separate hymns and, less significantly, the antiphons. These are, on one level, translations or paraphrases, as Crashaw drew from the Sarum Primers as the source for his texts.[6] But it is clear that Crashaw's indebtedness to the original is essentially a matter of content, not versification or style. One example will suffice. The Latin text for the hymn for the sixth hour reads:

Hora sexta Jesus est cruci conclavatus. Atq; cum latronibus pendens deputatus. Pre tormentis sitiens felle saturatus Agnus crimen diluit sic ludificatus.

The English version is similarly sparse:

The sixt hour springing before the midday, Jesu hand & foote to the cros thei nailed: With the shamefullest deth that they contrive mai And in despite betwene ii theeves him hanged. And for very paine when that he thursted, His thurst for to quench, they profered hym gal, This lambe thus illuded bought our sins al.[7]

Crashaw's version is an expansion, both in length and in metaphor, and the result is a poem much richer in meaning:

> Now is The noon of sorrow's night;
> High in his patience, as their spite,
> Lo the faint LAMB, with weary limb
> Beares that huge tree which must bear Him.
> That fatall plant, so great of fame
> For fruit of sorrow and of shame,
> Shall swell with both for HIM; and mix
> All woes into one CRUCIFIX.
> Is tortur'd Thirst, it selfe, too sweet a cup?

GALL, and more bitter mocks, shall make it up.
Are NAILES blunt pens of superficiall smart?
Contempt and scorn can send sure wounds to search the
                                              inmost Heart.

As George Williams has noted, the "Office" recalls Herbert's
"The Sacrifice," not just in subject but in tone as well.[8] In Herbert's
poem the speaker is Christ, hanging from the cross and both
remembering the events of Passion Week and reproaching those
listening. "The Sacrifice" frequently calls on the Christian mysteries and paradoxes so often found in Crashaw: Christ saving others
by not saving himself, the King condemned by His subjects, the
giver of life and breath condemned "with that same breath."
Herbert's poem is also liturgical in origin and, while less rigidly
organized than Crashaw's "Office," it reveals a similar development and theme.[9] There is no evidence that Crashaw was indebted
to Herbert's poem, however. Indeed, the prominence of the
subject in liturgy and church tradition virtually precludes such a
claim. It is nonetheless true that Crashaw's poem expounds on the
same events, often with similar effects.

The hymns of the "Office" take us through the seven devotional
hours and the events of the crucifixion day that occurred at those
times. The hymn for matins is introductory to the whole and recalls
in one image the theme of "Charitas Nimia." The betrayal and
capture of Christ is related in mercantile language: "The world's
price sett to sale, and by the bold/Merchants of Death and sin, is
bought and sold." The hymn for the hour of Prime recounts the
early summoning of Pilate and the cruelty of the accusers. The
hymn for the Third hour portrays the anger of the crowd and their
demands for Christ's death. In "The Sacrifice" Christ recalls the
outcries with a perception of the paradox: "Heark how they crie
aloud still, *Crucifie:/It is not fit he live a day,* they crie,/Who
cannot live lesse then eternally."[10] Crashaw also emphasizes the
inherent irony and paradox: "The Third hour's deafen'd with the
cry/Of crucify him, crucify./So goes the vote (nor ask them,
Why?)/Live Barabbas! and let GOD dy." In the hymn for the Sixth
hour, as cited above, Christ bears his own cross and is made to
drink the gall to quench His thirst. The hymn for the Ninth hour
speaks of the "awfull horror" of the death itself and its immediate
and chaotic effect on the earth through the darkened sun and
earthquakes. The final two hymns reveal differing reactions to

death. A soldier strikes the body in its side with a spear, but the Virgin, the "Great mother-maid," sits down to sing her Evensong (the "Stabat Mater Dolorosa") under a tree. In the last hymn Christ's body is anointed, and the speaker urges that his own Heart, not the borrowed grave, be the proper bed of Christ.

The hymns carry the reader progressively through the events leading to Christ's death and burial, neatly joining Hour and occasion for a heightened devotional effect. The antiphons characteristically emphasize the cross itself and the Christian paradoxes that help define the meaning of Christ's suffering and death: the cross is the tree that brings life from death, day from night; by His death and resurrection Christ freed a world once held captive by Death and thus captured Death itself; on the cross "LIFE seem'd to dy, DEATH dy'd indeed." The catalog of mysteries is most pronounced in the antiphon for Evensong, as Crashaw describes reactions to and effects of the death with a nearly oxymoronic impact: "Wofull"/"joyfull," "weep"/"sing," "TREE"/"THRONE," "yeilding"/"conquering." The tone of the final antiphon changes in keeping with the liturgical source; the poem is a more personal plea for salvation: "O save us then/Mercy-full KING of men!" The final Recommendation is also more personal and even glances momentarily at the ritual and poetic act of remembering there concluded: "That as I dedicate my de-voutest BREATH/To make a kind of LIFE for my lord's DEATH,/So from his living, and life-giving DEATH,/My dying LIFE may draw a new, and never fleeting BREATH."

II   *The Sacred and the Profane*

Since the "rediscovery" of the Metaphysicals in the early decades of the twentieth century, it has been fashionable to emphasize the connections between the seventeenth century and our own and to see the two eras similarly characterized by doubt, disruption, and alienation. The quintessential seventeenth-century poet, John Donne, for example, responds with ever-present uncertainty to a world where all is "in pieces, all cohærence gone;/All just supply, and all Relation."[11] While a perception of a "new philosophy" that calls much, if not "all," in doubt, is basic to an understanding of seventeenth-century mind and literature, it is easy to overstate the dis-ease of late Renaissance England in an attempt to associate that apparently troubled age with our own.

The fundamental belief in the unity of all created things may, to a Donne or Webster or even a Crashaw, no longer gain the easy acceptance that it held in sixteenth-century Elizabethan England, but the unity was characteristically asserted, explicitly and implicitly, nonetheless. It is seen in the Metaphysical aim to yoke heterogeneous ideas and images together, to join the homely with the elevated, the sacred with the profane. It is also seen in that singularly compelling aim of Baroque art to join the sensuous and the sacred in order better to attain the realm of God. In either tradition it is not outrageous or blasphemous to speak of the love of God for His creation in sexual terms, for the profane and sacred worlds, while apparently separate and distinct, are ultimately parts of a divinely created unity. It is a particular characteristic of the sacred vision of the Baroque that it both emphasizes the realm of the senses and strives to get beyond it. As Frank Warnke observes in a comment cited earlier, "The rich excess of sensuous imagery and the passionate expression of quasi-sexual emotion end in the affirmation of their opposite—the exclusive reality of the world of the spirit."[12]

Poem after poem from the *Carmen Deo Nostro* testifies to this perception of the profane and the sacred world and to a desire to use the one to advance to the other. No other theme is so apparent in Crashaw's sacred verse, and no other theme explains so much that is provocative and memorable or, alternately, forced and embarrassing. The cherub from "The Weeper" who sips a heavenly "breakfast" and indulges in a continuing heavenly aftertaste, and the several poems to ladies, from the unnamed M.R. to St. Teresa, who are urged in highly sexual language to yield to the sacred advances of God, all derive from the particular drive to unify experience by joining otherwise disparate realms.

The striking conjunction of the sensual and spiritual, the sacred and the profane, reaches its apex in the Teresa poems, where the divine ecstasy achieved by the saint is the result of a sacred love affair with God and serves as a model for spiritual union with God sought by the poet himself. In other poems, too, the juxtaposition of the sacred and the profane plays a vital, though often varying, role. These include "On Hope" and three poems addressed to women, the ode "On a prayer booke," "To the Same Party Councel concerning her Choise," and the Letter to the Countess of Denbigh.

"On Hope" is a joint composition of Crashaw and his Cambridge colleague Cowley, likely written while both were still at the university and consisting of four stanzas composed by Cowley, five by Crashaw. In the editions of *Steps* in 1646 and 1648, the poem was printed with alternating stanzas, beginning with one by Cowley. In the 1652 volume the stanzas by each poet are printed separately, the four by Cowley (titled "Hope") followed by the five by Crashaw ("M. Crashaws Answer For Hope").[13]

The original scheme of alternating stanzas reveals both the two directions of the poem and the close dependence of each of Crashaw's stanzas on the preceding one by Cowley for imagery and theme. Cowley argues his case against hope in a methodical and systematic way, showing it to be illusory, deceitful, and ultimately, "the most hopelesse thing of all." His is the reasoned argument of the "worldly philosopher."[14] Crashaw never neglects the imagery and theme introduced by Cowley but consistently rises above them, arguing the value of hope as a Christian philosopher. Cowley's verses are analytical and logical, dependent on analogy, hypotheses, and syllogistic reasoning to advance a conclusion that seems inevitably to follow from the evidence. Crashaw's verses are, characteristically, more exuberant and enthusiastic; he does not answer Cowley's logical argument but transcends it, converting Cowley's "profane metaphors . . . into sacred symbols"[15] and presenting the position of hope among the Christian hierarchical virtues of faith, hope, and love.

An example of Crashaw's use of Cowley's stanzas and his transcendence of them is seen in his response to Cowley's second verse. For Cowley, hope, the "bold taster of delight," is guilty of diminishing joys because it precedes them:

> Hope, thou bold taster of delight,
> Who, in stead of doing so, devour'st it quite
> Thou bring'st us an estate, yet leav'st us poore,
> By clogging it with Legacies before.
>   The joyes, which wee intire should wed,
>   Come deflour'd virgins to our bed.
> Good fortunes without gaine imported bee,
>   So mighty Custome's paid to thee.
> For joy, like Wine kept close, doth better taste:
> If it take ayre before, its spirits waste. (21–30)

Crashaw's response is contained in two stanzas. He retains image and language, even as immediately as the first line, but dismisses the earthly context in order to assert a heavenly one: "Thou art Loves Legacie under lock/Of Faith: the steward of our growing stocke" (31–32). Cowley's hope violates joy by preceding it; Crashaw's hope offers only a "chaste kisse":

> Nor will the Virgin-joyes wee wed
> Come lesse unbroken to our bed,
> Because that from the bridall cheeke of Blisse,
>   Thou thus steal'st downe a distant kisse,
> Hopes chaste kisse wrongs no more joyes maidenhead,
> Then Spousall rites prejudge the marriage-bed. (35–40)

Crashaw's second stanza in response to Cowley's works through the gustatory imagery that opens and closes Cowley's verse. Hope, to Cowley, is a "bold taster of delight"; to Crashaw, through hope "Young *Time* is taster to Eternity." Cowley's joy, like wine, is threatened with spoilage because it is anticipated and preceded by hope. Crashaw's hope is a "generous wine [that] with age growes strong, not sower." It is, above all, a virtue whose essence is irrevocably joined to love:

> Thy golden head never hangs downe,
> Till in the lap of Loves full noone
> It falls, and dyes: oh no, it melts away
>   As doth the dawne into the day:
> As lumpes of Sugar lose themselves, and twine
> Their subtile essence with the soule of Wine. (45–50)

The pattern of Crashaw's response seen here is characteristic of the rest of the poem. His strategy is to take language and image from Cowley but alter them, electing not to answer Cowley on his terms (in spite of the implications of the 1652 title) but to create a new and theological context within which he may advance to a new and sacred understanding. Furthermore, Crashaw heightens his poetic aim through the exuberance of tone and the excitement of paradox. For the most part Cowley avoids both, for neither fits comfortably into his mode of reasoned argument. To Cowley's simple "Hope" Crashaw responds with "Deare Hope!," "Faire Hope!," "Sweet *Hope*!," and, in the final stanza, "*Faith's* Sister! Nurse of faire desire!/Feares Antidote!." When Cowley accuses hope of being a cheat, Crashaw transforms accusation to paradox: "kind cheat! faire fallacy! by thee/Wee are not where, or what wee bee,/But what, and where wee would bee: thus art thou/Our absent presence, and our future now" (67–70).

Cowley's poem is, finally, the cry of Nature, where reason and order and understanding prevail; Crashaw's poem promotes other values—faith, hope, love—that go beyond reason and thus cannot fully answer the complaints of reason. Crashaw speaks from the world of Grace, which at once includes and transcends Nature, as his final lines confirm: "Truè *Hope's* a glorious Huntresse, and her chase/The God of Nature in the field of Grace" (89–90).

The Ode on a Prayer Book, "To the Same Party," and the Letter to the Countess of Denbigh can be joined by a fourth, "On Mr. G. Herberts booke intituled the Temple," to form a quartet of poems addressed to women contemporary with Crashaw. They may, furthermore, be seen as part of a larger group of poems written about, or developed through the perspective of, a woman: notably, the elegies on St. Alexis, "The Weeper," the hymns on the Virgin, and the Teresa poems.

The least representative poem is also the shortest. Crashaw's poem accompanying Herbert's *The Temple* is a simple, modest, and graceful tribute both to Herbert and to the woman. The "Divinest love" of Herbert's book will join with the "well perfumed prayer" of the woman to send her daily to heaven. The other three poems addressed to women reveal some intriguing similarities and some significant variations on one basic theme: the woman should yield to the advances of God her lover.

The most restrained of the three poems is "To the Same Party." In the 1648 and 1652 volumes it follows the ode "On a prayer booke sent to Mrs. M.R.," a woman who has not been identified. The basis for the second poem is apparently the woman's disappointment following an unsuccessful love match. The poet seizes the moment to speak for the higher intentions of his "dearer LORD." The love offered to the woman in the past is from a profane, secular world— "this lower sphear/Of froth and bubbles" (8–9). It is love (and potential lovers) captured as "Peacocks and Apes,/Illustrious flyes,/Guilded dunghills, glorious LYES,/ . . . Oathes of water, words of wind" (12–17). In sum, the love of the "son[s] of dust." The poet urges a response to a "braver love" that will put the lady in the company of the "fair sonnes of fire." Her disappointment in

human love was, in fact, part of the "high strategem" of her new
and "Mighty lover/Of soules":

> It was his heavnly art
> Kindly to crosse you
> In your mistaken love,
> That, at the next remove
> Thence he might tosse you
> And strike your troubled heart
Home to himself. (45–51)

Her present sorrow is thus a more intimate version of the *felix
culpa*, a "Happy Mystake" that leads her from unfulfilled love
among the realms of men to an eternal love from a "farre more
worthy SPOUSE."

The poet uses but does not elaborate on the biblical imagery of
Christ as the bridegroom and his followers as his betrothed. The
language is largely devoid of any overt sexuality or any semblance
of ecstasy in love, urging instead a more reasoned, though no less
significant, decision to unite with God. Crashaw himself has a role
rather unlike those he assumes in related poems; he is both the
spokesman for his lord and a confidante of the lady. He alerts her
to the realities of a profane love, hints at the expectations of divine
love, and then, as a kind of innocent tattletale, reveals the secret
plan of his lord to win the lady for himself. The final lines of the
poem imply not only the seriousness of the decision but also the
modesty of the poet in making this counsel: "o when you choose
agen/May it not be amongst the sonnes of Men" (58–59).

Quite different in effect, although similar in its primary image, is
the other poem to "M.R.," the ode accompanying a prayer book.
The poem is in two versions, the first printed in 1646, the second in
1648 and 1652, but the changes are slight and not very significant.
As in "To the Same Party," the woman addressed here is urged to
forsake all earthly loves and to accept God as her lover; but the
sensuality inherent in the image, only glanced at in the other poem,
is here explored and exploited to the fullest. An important reason
for the difference in tone and impact is found in the decisive
influences that lie behind this poem: St. Teresa, the Song of Songs,
and Thomas Carew's "A Rapture." A. F. Allison has shown that the
poem is "Crashaw's most successful description of the mystical
progress of the soul," and that, more specifically, it follows the

three stages of the mystical life as outlined by St. Teresa in her *Interior Castle*: Purgation, involving "self-mortification," "meditation," and "prayer" (lines 1–64); Illumination, involving "purification," "grace," and "intellectual enlightenment" (lines 65–86); and Union, involving the "perfect conformity of the will," the "re-creation of self in God" (lines 87–124).[16] Allison demonstrates, furthermore, that while the final section of the ode reveals the influence of Teresa and her borrowings from the Song of Songs, its particular indebtedness is to a much more worldly source, "the most notoriously licentious verses" of "A Rapture."[17]

The conjunction of such diverse sources in this poem addressed to a woman results in a remarkable explosion of sensuality and ecstasy that mirrors the mystical progress that is the poem's subject. The poem begins more modestly, although even there sensuous potentiality is explored more than it was in the previous poem: the prayer book is a "nest of new-born sweets" surrounded by the "comly bands" of the lady's hands; it is "love's great artillery" that, contracted, "comes to ly/Close couch't in your white bosom" (16–17). The poet reminds the lady that the bride of Christ must be pure and faithful; the "loytering HEART" that dallies "Among the gay mates of the god of flyes" will find that it has lost its favored position with the "noble BRIDEGROOM." Throughout the first section the poet calls for the action appropriate to the first stage of the mystical progress of the soul: humility, self-denial, prayer.

The second stage of the progress is described in language from the mystical tradition, but with no particular exploitation of its sexual associations. The lady is reminded of what the faithless heart will miss: "hidden sweets and holy joyes," "WORDS which are not heard with EARES," "Amorous languishments," "luminous trances," "SIGHTS which are not seen with eyes," "Delicious DEATHS," "soft exalations/Of soul," "a hundred thousand goods, glories, and graces." The first two parts of the ode are not so different in tone and effect from the whole of "To the Same Party"; we are aware of sexual associations lying just beneath the surface of the language but seldom are they given prominence.

In the final section, however, profane sensuality and spiritual ecstasy are joined in a kind of sacred "rapture." Prior to the final stage Crashaw acknowledges the inadequacy of language to capture the mystical experience: union with God includes "many a mystick thing/ . . . For which it is no shame/That dull mortality must not know a name" (82–86). Names are not given in the final section, but understanding is acquired through analogy: God is reached, or at least approached, through the senses, and the language of the poem confirms the unity of soul with God, of profane with sacred. The "fair soul" receives the "pretious sweets" of her God-Lover; she "Makes hast to meet her morning spouse/ And close with his immortall kisses" (102–103); she seizes "her sweet prey/All fresh and fragrant as he rises/Dropping with a baulmy Showr/A delicious dew of spices" (107–10). She will, furthermore, encounter "ten thousand paradises," "the rich and roseall spring of those rare sweets," "Bottomles treasures/Of pure inebriating pleasures," and will experience "How many Heav'ns at once it is/To have her GOD become her LOVER" (123–24).

The most impressive of the poems written to contemporary women is the Letter to the Countess of Denbigh. In this poem Crashaw speaks as a Roman convert, urging the wavering and uncertain countess to follow a similar action, to, as the 1652 version puts it, "render her selfe without further delay into the Communion of the Catholick Church." The poem exists in two versions, and they are importantly diverse at points. The original version was printed as the lead poem in *Carmen Deo Nostro* and is a kind of extension of the dedication of the volume to "My Lady the Countesse of Denbigh by Her most devoted Servant. R.C. In hearty acknowledgment of his immortall obligation to her Goodnes & Charity."[18] The poem later appeared separately in a pamphlet, printed in London probably in 1653. The second version is over twenty lines longer, is less immediately engaging and less personal, and takes the personal circumstance of the countess as a basis for commenting more thoroughly on the theme of yielding to love's advances.

Through the first twenty lines the two versions are not significantly different, although the 1652 poem is preceded by an emblem depicting a heart with a lock on it and a brief epigram setting the theme of the longer poem:

> 'Tis not the work of force but skill
> To find the way into man's will.
> 'Tis love alone can hearts unlock.
> Who knowes the WORD, he needs not knock.

The epigram points to the problem and the resolution presented in the poem: the heart is undecided and hesitant and must, to be committed, open to the wooing of love.

In the opening lines the "Heav'n-beseiged Heart" . . . /Stands Trembling at the Gate of Blisse" (1–2). The poet initially expresses surprise and bewilderment more than dismay or anger; his several questions in the first twenty lines indicate the attitude of a friend who is honestly concerned but sincerely perplexed:

> What Fatall, yet fantastick, Bands
> Keep the free Heart from his own Hands?
> Say, lingring Fair, why comes the Birth
> Of your brave Soul so slowly forth? (13–16)

Both versions introduce an analogy from nature to underscore the danger of the lady's continuing irresolution. She will become the victim of her own indecision, just as "when the Year takes cold we see/Poor Waters their own Prisoners be:/Fetter'd and lock'd up fast they lie/In a cold self-captivity" (21–24).

The 1652 version retains the personal emphasis from this point on, calling on "Allmighty LOVE" to "end this long warr" of indecision and doubt, to "fix this fair INDEFINITE," to "choose out that sure decisive dart/Which has the Key of this close heart,/Knowes all the corners of't, and can controul/The self-shutt cabinet of an unsearcht soul" (33–36). Love is the active force through the middle section of the earlier poem, making its conquest, raising the "tall Trophee of [its] Powre," and proceeding so as to "kill this rebell-word, IRRESOLUTE." In the quasi-military/sexual imagery of the poem, it is the woman's role to be passive, to yield to the advances of power and love. Her "peevish strength/Of weaknes" will come to a resolution; she will "hast to drink the wholesome dart"; she will "Meet it with wide-spread armes; and see/It's seat your soul's just center be" (41–56).

Having described the participants in the military and sexual encounter, the poet finally urges a capitulation that is, paradoxically, a victory. In this conflict it is "cowardise that keeps this feild/And want of courage not to yeild" (61–62). The final lines diminish the sexual undertones of the imagery and heighten the military associations. They are reminiscent of the opening image of Donne's "Batter my heart, three-personed God," and, indeed, the conjunction of military and sexual metaphors in both poems speaks to a similar theme and tradition. Here it is the woman (or her heart) who is the Fort that must yield to love. As Satan threatened capture in Donne's poem, the danger here is that indecision will lead the woman to be "Death's prey." Thus, her failure to convert will result both in the rejection of love and in her own undoing.

Richard Strier calls the 1653 version of the letter "more characteristic" of Crashaw and, in the final analysis, "inferior and far less interesting."[19] His principal emphasis is on the more personal tone of the earlier version and its qualities of tension and doubt, features he finds lacking in the 1653 version and in the majority of Crashaw's poems. Those characteristics aside, however, the earlier version is in a number of ways *more* typical and, certainly, more allied in theme and imagery with other Crashaw poems than is the 1653 poem. The influence of St. Teresa is more apparent in the original, and the consistent working through of the military and sexual associations identifies that version with the poems on the Spanish saint.

Lines 27–77 of the second version are virtually unmatched by anything in the original. They begin after the assertion of the danger of self-captivity, but, rather than speaking directly of the woman's irresolution as the first version does, they portray more generally and more theoretically the message of the poem: it is in the nature of things to act and to respond to love. In its elaboration on this theme the 1653 poem is perhaps more obviously Baroque even though language and imagery are moderate in tone and impact.

Love, the poet claims, is slow to move only the woman's heart; in all other things, fulfillment follows the offer of promise: "Each mindfull Plant hasts to make good/The hope and promise of his Bud" (35–36). Winds, waves, even metals and stones reveal their response to love by acting in accordance with Nature's laws. It is therefore more surprising that humankind, alone among created things to be wooed by God, hesitates and resists His active attempts. The lines of the poem immediately prior to the resolution are more openly theological and form the rational basis for the poet's later plea:

> When love of Us call'd Him to see
> If wee'd vouchsafe his company,
> He left his Father's Court, and came

> Lightly as a Lambent Flame,
> Leaping upon the Hills, to be
> The Humble King of You and Me. (67–72)

The final appeal in the earlier version follows a series of highly charged images drawn from sexual and military conquest, and the response invited is a decisive emotional commitment. The language of the appeal in the second version is very nearly the same, but it has lost its immediacy and energy because of the extended and sometimes gratuitous discussion that precedes it. The long middle section of the 1653 letter is not irrelevant but it is too distant in tone and aim for good effect. The focus of the original has been sacrificed in the attempt to persuade the woman through analogy and natural principles, and the allusions to flowers and fruits, to winds and waters, to the doves drawing Venus's chariot, and finally to the Incarnation itself result in a blurred and confusing perspective. In an attempt to give his appeal a broader naturalistic and theological base, Crashaw has forsaken the poem's most impressive quality: the unyielding appeal to one woman's heart to open itself to love and commitment.

III *"The Weeper"*

It is likely that, with the possible exception of the infamous epigram "Blessed be the paps," "The Weeper" is better known than any other Crashaw poem.[20] It is consistently anthologized (or parts of it are), and it has received much critical attention, not all of it, certainly, favorable. The unofficial endorsement of "The Weeper" as a particularly representative Crashaw poem has led not a few readers to remember Crashaw as the author of some unusual and excessive lines, notably those in which the Magdalen's tears are described as "two faithfull fountaines;/Two walking baths; two weeping motions;/Portable, and compendious oceans."

Many previous comments on "The Weeper" are misleading, I think, in three ways. First, because "The Weeper" sometimes exhibits a loose sense of structure and development, the poem is said to have no organizing principle at all; it is, Praz asserts, "little more than a rosary of epigrams or madrigals clumsily linked together, without progression."[21] I would argue, on the contrary, that there are image clusters that provide an organizing principle to the poem and that some sequences are crucial and inviolable if the poem is to work as intended. The two other tendencies among critical reactions are related: "The Weeper" is frequently cited as a poem typical of Crashaw or, alternately, typical of the Baroque. Not surprisingly, the first judgment most often accompanies a larger condemnation of certain elements of what is perceived as the Crashavian style; Robert Adams, for example, points to "The Weeper" (as well as "Blessed be the paps") as evidence of the "bad taste" to be found in Crashaw's verse.[22] And the second judgment implies a negative response toward the Baroque and its impact as an artistic style.

It is mistaken, I am convinced, to accept a single-minded notion of the "typical" Crashavian style or to believe that the Baroque is grotesque extravagance or incongruous elaboration, qualities that have been associated with "The Weeper." Simply put, I do not believe that "The Weeper" is particularly typical of Crashaw *or* the Baroque; it is no more fair to single it out as representative of Crashaw than it is to endorse Donne's "Hymn to God the Father" as typical of his wit or, to cite a radically different example, Faulkner's *Sanctuary* as typical of his themes and action. Extremes do not yield paradigms or patterns. Helen White wisely observed a number of years ago that "the piling up of rhapsodic images in 'The Weeper' has blinded readers and critics" to the more logical structure of much of Crashaw's verse, that, in fact, "the line of development of the usual Crashaw poem is as firm, basically, as the line of a baroque statue or building, and the logical mass as substantial."[23]

The negative criticism notwithstanding, "The Weeper" is not so utterly indefensible as some have implied, and we are wrong to dismiss it too readily.[24] In considering "The Weeper," as all know but few have emphasized, we have not one poem but two, and, as with the Letter to the Countess of Denbigh, the two versions lead at times to two very different poems.[25] The 1646 version was included in the first edition of *Steps to the Temple*; a revised version appeared in the 1648 volume and is, with the exception of a few minor changes, the poem also printed in 1652. In 1646 and 1648 "The Weeper" was joined by "The Teare," which appears to be an early, and brief, poetic essay into some of the themes and images explored in greater abundance in the longer poem. A comparison of the two substantive versions of "The Weeper" provides an answer to the consummate objection raised against the fragmented nature of the poem, an objection, as voiced by Praz, that "what is lacking is a central point round which the poem should gravitate in a harmonious coordination of its parts."[26] It is precisely this central point which has been added to the second version of the poem and which indicates Crashaw's perception of the weakness of the first.

Crashaw's 1646 "Weeper," though without the structural center of the later version, hardly fits Praz's description of a "clumsily linked" rosary. There are, throughout the poem, thematic and image clusters that not only link one stanza to another but also join one image cluster to others which follow or precede it. After the opening salutation to the Magdalen's eyes, the poet takes us upward as the tears, though seeming to fall, are paradoxically shown to rise toward a heavenly destination.[27] The image cluster first appears in stanza two, as the eyes, which have in the previous stanza been variously "Sister Springs," "Parents of Silver-forded rills," "Ever bubling things," "Thawing Christall," and "Snowy Hills," now become Heavens as the tears become "ever-falling stars." Because the tears are so "pretious" their only appropriate destination is heaven, where they join other waters among the "milky rivers" (the Milky Way). The superiority of the tears to other heaven-bound streams is seen as the tears become the "Creame" which is in turn sipped by a "briske Cherub" of heaven who is able to taste of this "breakefast all day long." Stanza six concludes the focus on heaven and the image cluster begun in stanza two (stars-stream-cream-breakfast) by converting the breakfast cream into wine for a feast, an appropriate conversion since the solitary occasion in stanza five, involving a single cherub, becomes the great celebration in honor of a "new bright guest" in heaven. There is extravagance here, of course, but nothing fails to fit. Setting the poem in heaven at the beginning emphasizes the symbolic value of the tears as a sign of devout penitence and as a source (because they are an example) of further spiritual nourishment.

The progression to stanza seven is abrupt but not without cause. Having asserted the divine value of the tears, Crashaw recognizes their earthly context as well. The following nine stanzas, therefore, take images from Nature, showing the greater worth of the Magdalen's tears. The dew would leave its privileged position on a primrose or a lily if it could be a tear (st. 7); the gold from the amber-weeping tree is not half so rich as the tear-drops (st. 8); the tears are sorrow's "richest Pearles" (st. 9); they are more valued

than medicinal balsam (sts. 12 and 13) and are superior, in their
silver richness, to the golden stream of the river Tagus (st. 14). And
finally, the tears are as the showers of April that anticipate the
flowers of May, exemplified here by the blushing redness of the
Magdalen's cheeks. All of the objects that yield images in these
stanzas are highly valued. The primrose is the flower of the Virgin,
the lily, of Christ; similarly, the golden amber, the pearl, the
medicinal balsam, and the golden waters of Tagus are rare and
costly. Yet the tears are worth more.

An allegorical portrait of sorrow and sadness sits in the middle of
these images drawn from Nature (sts. 9–11), and it distorts the
focus of the poem at this stage. Otherwise Crashaw's aim is
consistent, and stanza 15, coming at the end of this section,
provides an effective transition between the focus on Nature
which precedes it and the concern with Time which follows:

> Well does the *May* that lyes
> Smiling in thy cheekes, confesse,
> The *April* in thine eyes,
> Mutuall sweetnesse they expresse.
> No *April* e're lent softer showres,
> Nor *May* returned fairer flowers.

April and May are appropriate representations of natural occur-
rences, identified then and now with the frequency of rain and the
blooming of flowers; but they are, as months, measures of time and
hence lead into the final image cluster of the poem. The important
measure of time in the poem is the rhythmic falling of the tears, and
that measure is more accurate than other and more conventional
timepieces ("Hower-Glasses," cadences in music, or Night, days,
months, and years). The tears are seen, more importantly, as a
measure of the Magdalen's life:

> Not, so long she liv'd,
> Will thy tombe report of thee
> But *so long she greiv'd*,
> Thus must we date thy memory.
> Others by Dayes, by Monthes, by Yeares
> Measure their Ages, Thou by Teares. (st. 20)

Of the final three stanzas in the poem, the first two are an address to the tears, the last the response. The significance of the tears is reiterated in these stanzas as the poet affirms that a great enticement must be leading them from "her eyes swolne wombes of sorrow." In view of the bold and extensive imagery that has informed the portrayal of the tears to this point, the final response is effectively low-key:

> We goe not to seeke
> The darlings of *Aurora's* bed,
> The Roses modest cheeke
> Nor the Violets humble head.
> No such thing; we goe to meet
> A worthier object, *Our Lords* feet.

"The Weeper" is thus arranged so as to provide some sense of unity among stanzas. There are distinct groupings, in other words, even though we can hardly claim that the total poem must be arranged as it is to be aesthetically satisfying. (Crashaw himself gave the lie to that assumption by his own rearrangement.) There is an appropriate, though not inevitable, development as we move from the opening address to the eyes (1) to the setting in heaven (2-6), back down to earth and natural scenes (7-8, 12-15), to a consideration of Time and timelessness (16-20), and finally to the address to and response of the tears themselves (21-23). It remains true, nonetheless, that a reader, perceiving no central focus in the poem, is hard pressed to see it progressing organically within a unified whole.

Of the several types of changes in the 1648 "Weeper," the crucial one is the addition of eight consecutive stanzas not found in the original.[28] Beginning in stanza 15 and continuing through stanza 22, Crashaw gives his poem, quite literally, a new center. Praz has argued that the second version shows no improvement over the first; an anonymous writer in TLS goes even further, asserting that the "lack of any development of thought is . . . fully shown in the later expanded version where ten new stanzas are added and the original ones are redistributed. . . . [Crashaw] has such small powers of self-criticism that the added verses include phrases that repel more than any in the earlier version; it would be cruel to quote them."[29] This writer is correct, of course, in emphasizing the added stanzas, but I would contend, contrary to the usual judgment, that the stanzas are effectively presented, that they give a new and valuable emphasis to the devotional basis of the poem, and that they provide the element Praz found missing in the original, "a central point round which the poem . . . gravitate[s] in a harmonious coordination of its parts."

In his study of Lope de Vega and the tradition of Magdalen poems, Perry J. Powers notes that one of the unique features of Crashaw's poem is that there is no narrative of the saint's life and no full-bodied portrait of Mary.[30] Rather, her tears are given significance as the sign and symbol of the value and power of Christian penitence. There is a hint of narrative and of her personal role, however, in the central stanzas of the poem, the ones added by Crashaw in the second version. These stanzas, furthermore, focus on the unique role of Christ in the Magdalen's life (and thus his central role in the redemptive aim of the poem) and on the abiding paradoxes that define her life and her relationship to Christ. The added stanzas become the penitential and emblematic center of the poem, recalling as they do the traditional view of the Magdalen as penitent sinner and reminding us of the emblem that accompanies the second version, where the tears of the Magdalen's eyes clash paradoxically but meaningfully with her inflamed heart. The stanzas expound on the paradoxes that inform the change in Mary (and hence the change in all penitent sinners) and emphasize the central action of Christ as both lamb and shepherd, as sacrifice and master.

Rather than being arbitrarily inserted at this point in the poem, the central stanzas are particularly apt and coherent, and Crashaw skillfully joins the sequence to previously written stanzas that precede and follow it. Stanza 14 has hinted at the paradox implicit in the Magdalen's face, as April and May, showers and flowers, are joined in one "Mutuall sweetnesse." Stanza 15 speaks to the paradox more emphatically:

> O cheeks! Bedds of chast loves
> By your own showres seasonably dash't;
> Eyes! nests of milky doves
> In your own wells decently washt,
> O wit of love! that thus could place
> Fountain and Garden in one face.

Beginning with this stanza Crashaw balances what has been an almost exclusive emphasis on the Magdalen's sadness, the sorrow in her penitence, as indicated by her tears. Now he reminds us that

love, not sadness, is to be the dominant note.[31] It is appropriate that
the previous stanza describes May as "*Smiling* in thy cheeks," for
here those same cheeks are the beds of "chast loves" that indicate
the fruition and intention of the Magdalen's life. Only through the
"wit of love" can the conjunction of weeping and joy, fountain and
garden, be accomplished. The paradoxical joining of "kind
contrarietyes" is continued in the next two stanzas, as woes and
loves, tears and smiles, kissing and confuting, rain and sunshine,
floods and fires are "Mixt and made freinds by love's sweet
powres."

This central paradox was only hinted at in the earlier version.
There the mention of April and May suggested contrary appearances on the Magdalen's face, but it served primarily to introduce
the concern with Time. Now the paradox itself is emphasized as it
lies at the heart of all penitential experiences, of which Mary's is a
supreme example. The added concern with love cannot go
unnoticed, as each stanza stresses the word (it has not appeared
before in the poem) and its power as a motivating and unifying
force.

Crashaw's focus on "love's sweet powres" leads inevitably to the
ultimate source of love: Christ. Nowhere else in the poem, except
for the very last line, are we aware of Christ's presence. But here, in
conjunction with the focus on love, his appearance is fitting. He is a
sacred Cupid whose arrow has struck the heart of Mary and who
has caused both the inflamed heart and the weeping eyes. And
Crashaw reminds us again of the quality of love that produces such
effects; other loves are shallow exhibitions in contrast to the love
that guides Mary's heart: "Vain loves avant! bold hands forbear!/
The lamb hath dipp't his white foot here."

Stanza 19 has provoked frequent negative comment, most of it
directed against those particularly liquid images through which
Crashaw describes the eyes of the weeping Mary following Christ:
"two faithfull fountaines;/Two walking baths; two weeping
motions;/Portable and compendious oceans." The images are
clearly excessive, but that, of course, is intended in order to
demonstrate the extreme penitence of Mary. Nonetheless, the
images are too overdrawn to be effective, and they may, furthermore, blind us to the fact that this stanza is more specifically
located than any other, with the possible exception of the last. For a
brief moment we glimpse the lamb of the previous stanza straying
along the familiar biblical path of Christ, followed always by the
woman whom, by love, he has changed. There is the added

suggestion of Christ as both lamb and shepherd, as the pure sacrifice whose redemptive act made possible Mary's penitence and the master now leading one of his flock.

The final three stanzas of the new sequence continue the balanced concern with Christ and the Magdalen, for their action and interaction are the core of the devotional nature of the poem. Indeed, in stanza 20 we are reminded of the encounter between Mary and Christ that is further imaged in the concluding stanza. The weeping of Mary is one of the riches of Christ just as, in a more concrete manner, she reveals that wealth by washing His feet with her "Sylver" tears and wiping them with her "Gold" hair. The silver and gold of tears and hair are enlarged in the next stanza to become "a wandring mine,/A voluntary mint, that strowes/Warm sylver shoures where're he goes." Throughout these stanzas and the one that follows the relationship between the penitent sinner and the loving Savior is a reciprocal one. The love of the Savior leads to the penitence of the sinner; that penitence is, in turn, wealth and replenishment for Him. The very existence of the sinner's tears confirms and enhances the wealth of this particular Prince.

The final stanza in the added group concentrates more exactly on the weeper herself, here seen, in yet another variation of the central paradox, as a "pretious Prodigall." The ceaseless wasting of tears is a kind of wasting of herself (hence, *"Mercilesse* love"), a sign of her willingness to expend herself entirely by her sorrow ("thy measure . . . is all"). Stanza 22, while focusing on the Magdalen, implicitly directs us to Christ as well. Her willing gift of her devotion and repentance is a mirror of the more encompassing gift of Christ, and the "Mercilesse love" that emanates from her is an ironic recollection of the merciful love of the Savior. The merciless love that is measured in the endless stream of tears leads us to another measure: Time. The tears, by their very constancy, measure time, and by their endless flowing suggest eternity: "All places, Times, and objects be/Thy teare's sweet opportunity."

The one later addition to the poem, stanza 27, gives us a final view of the paradox governing the poem, the joining of sorrow and love through the images of heat and water, flame and flood. The continual flowing of the tears is viewed as the expiration of moisture as a result of heat:

> So doe perfumes expire.
> So sigh tormented sweets, opprest
> With proud unpittying fire.

> Such Teares the suffring Rose that's vext
> With ungentle flames does shed,
> Sweating in a too warm bed.

Richness is imaged here both materially (perfumes, sweets) and symbolically ("the suffring Rose") and is effectively united with the conjunction of water and flame. Without explicit statement the stanza encourages us to recall that the source of the tears is the wounded, inflamed heart that has been forever affected by "love's sweet powres." With the final attention to the inflamed heart of love that produces the tears of sorrow, we are prepared to witness the "worthy object" of their flowing: "our lord's FEET."

It goes without saying that "The Weeper" is far from a perfect poem or a thoroughly satisfying one. In spite of growing evidence that most of Crashaw's images are more traditional than bizarre or grotesque, some notable examples are too self-conscious, too excessive and drawn out to be easily read and appreciated. The arrangement of the poem is not, however, so capricious as some have suggested. It does not move through a systematic or logical development but through clusters of images, through an associative, rather than logical and intellectual progression. Beyond this, the major stanzas added by Crashaw in the second version seem not to have been given their just due. In them we see a concentration lacking in the earlier version. The central paradox of the weeping eyes and flaming heart, pointing to both the sinner and the Savior, is introduced, reiterated and enhanced throughout this central portion and repeated in a later stanza (27). It provides, furthermore, an added balance that is crucial in this poem on a penitent sinner. The first version focuses almost entirely on sorrow and sadness, giving added emphasis to that dimension through an allegorical representation of those emotions. The second version includes that part of the penitential act but eliminates the allegory and reminds us of the love and the lamb that complete the gift of grace. Thematically the poem is more attractive and balanced, and structurally more coherent and unified. A usual judgment of "The Weeper" is that it has moments of brilliance with little overall coherence. It seems to me, rather, to fluctuate between moments of brilliance and moments of disappointing extravagance but to reveal throughout a sensible coherence and unity.

CHAPTER 5

The Major Hymns

"**H**YMNUS scitis quid est?" Do you know, poses St. Augustine, what a hymn is? His answer emphasizes three essential elements: it is a song of praise for God ("Hymnus ergo tria habet, et cantum et laudem et Dei").[1] Without any one of the three there can be no hymn. Puttenham also comments on the hymn tradition, identifying the crucial elements previously isolated by St. Augustine. Pagan gods, he says, were honored "by their Poetes in hymnes, which is an extraordinarie and divine praise, extolling and magnifying them for their great powers and excellencie of nature in the highest degree of laude." The qualities Puttenham sees in pagan hymns—"extraordinarie and divine praise," "the highest degree of laude"—are exemplified in Christian hymns as well. Indeed, he is quick to argue the virtue and efficacy of Christian hymns as opposed to their pagan counterparts. Extraordinary praise of a pagan god is essentially misguided and fruitless; the "highest degree of laude" is best reserved for "the God of the Christians, [since] such divine praise might be verified."[2]

For the Christian poet there were important and diverse biblical examples of the hymn, from the searching, introspective meditations of some of the Psalms to the emotional and erotic enthusiasm of the Song of Songs. The tradition of passionate language of praise found its justification and origin in the Song of Songs, where sensuousness, joy, and a religious-sexual ecstasy combine in an uninhibited celebration of the joys of divine, yet still erotic, union.[3]

The poetic qualities implicit in the hymn tradition, one source of which is the Song of Songs, are evident in Crashaw's final poems, especially the festive hymns and paraphrases and the hymns to St. Teresa. The "exclamatory, ecstatic tone" of many of the poems has been explained by the fact that Crashaw was a Roman convert, and thus excited by his new discovery or, alternately, that the "sweet inebriated ecstasy" was inborn, a trait natural and inevitable for Crashaw.[4] Neither view seems satisfactory, the first ignoring the difficulties of dating the poems and contradicting the evidence of ecstatic rhetoric that apparently precedes Crashaw's conversion, the second emphasizing too much a quality found principally in Crashaw's later works and neglecting some very different strains in other of his secular and religious verse. The tradition of praise and celebration found a rich seedbed in the temperament of Crashaw, and he added to that tradition his own passionate and eloquent voice. The mature Crashaw transcended the plain and Metaphysical styles of some of his earlier poetry, not so much because the Baroque voice was inborn but because it was that voice that, most of all, he nurtured. His decision to write hymns, to celebrate the joys of Christian holy days, to give voice to the meaning of the Nativity or the Epiphany, or to revel in the profound influence of St. Teresa and her mystical ecstasy, all reflect the poetic sensibility and religious temperament of a man who was making the pilgrimage from Canterbury to Rome. Whether or not he is formally a convert at the occasion of writing is less significant than the inescapable conclusion from the poems themselves: his commitment, as Anglican or as Roman, is to a celebration of a God who can best be reached through the enthusiastic affirmation and proclamation of sacred truths. The God celebrated in the hymns is a Baroque God who is approached through the fullest realization of the senses.

The hymns to be discussed here include five of Crashaw's creation and six paraphrases of medieval hymns. The five original hymns are the Hymn to the Name of Jesus, the Hymn in the Holy Nativity, the Hymn for New Year's Day ("the Circumcision day of our Lord"), the Hymn in the Glorious Epiphanie, and the Hymn in the Glorious Assumption. The paraphrases are those of the "Vexilla Regis" ("The Hymn of the Holy Crosse"), "Sancta Maria Dolorum" ("The Mother of Sorrows"), "Adoro Te" ("The Hymn of Sainte Thomas in Adoration of the Blessed Sacrament"), "Lauda Sion Salvatorem" ("The Hymn for the Bl. Sacrament"), "Dies Iræ Dies Illa" ("The Hymn of the Church, in Meditation of the Day of Judgment"), and "O Gloriosa Domina." Although these eleven poems and paraphrases vary considerably among themselves they are united in their consistent manifestation of a more passionate

eloquence, a figured and repetitive style, and a Baroque sensibility
that carries a reader by rhetorical waves toward the object of
praise and contemplation.

I The Paraphrases of Medieval Hymns

Among Crashaw's paraphrases of medieval hymns, even those
less noticeably altered from the originals, three new or newly
emphasized qualities are most pronounced: the subjective and
dynamic involvement of the speaker, a richer and more developed
pattern of imagery, and a more emotional, more exclamatory
tone.[5] Crashaw takes the relative plainness and directness of the
Latin verse and adds complexity, subjectivity, and greater
emotion. The explanatory heading accompanying the "Sancta
Maria Dolorum" is relevant to a lesser or greater extent to each of
the paraphrases; each is "a Pathetical descant upon the devout
Plainsong" of the original.[6] To melody is added harmony, to the
straight line is added the wave, the angle, the circle.

One approach to the paraphrases is by their relative faithfulness
to the original. With this criterion we find that there are essentially
two groups of three. The two paraphrases of St. Thomas, "Adoro
Te" and "Lauda Sion Salvatorem," and the paraphrase of "Dies Iræ
Dies Illa" are fairly close renderings of the originals, although each
reveals significant changes as well; the versions of "Vexilla Regis,"
"Sancta Maria Dolorum," and "O Gloriosa Domina" exhibit
increasing freedom from the style and impact of the originals,
leading to varied accents and themes, if not entirely different
poems. What was suggested about Crashaw's earliest translations
is equally true of his later ones: no single "theory" of translation
controls his response to existing poetic material. He *may* translate
fairly closely but he does not feel compelled to. In these works, as
in earlier writings, he reveals the capacity to follow Denham's
advice to avoid the "vulgar error" of being unimaginatively *"fidus
interpres."*[7]

St. Thomas Aquinas is the likely author of "Adoro Te" and the
certain author of "Lauda Sion Salvatorem."[8] It may be significant
that Crashaw chose to follow closely the dominant themes, images,
and, especially, the pattern of development in the Latin hymns of
this most important and influential medieval saint. He added his
own distinct touches but not so much that the original could not
readily be seen in the translation.

The "Adoro Te" in the Latin is a prayer to be said after Mass, and celebrates the God who is hidden within the sacramental forms ("Quae sub his figuris vere latitas").[9] The poet acknowledges the importance of faith that can be gained only by hearing ("auditu") and compares his state to that of the repentant thief on the cross and the apostle Thomas. Both came to profess a faith that the poet seeks in greater abundance ("Fac me tibi semper magis credere"), and he prays that through the bread and wine of the sacraments he may perceive the hidden presence of Christ, an anticipation of the experience of the full revelation of God's glory ("Visu sim beatus tuæ gloriæ").

The seven quatrains of the original are matched by seven stanzas of varying length in Crashaw's poem, but the total effect is that of a sparse twenty-eight-line poem turned into a more elaborate version of exactly double the length.[10] The pattern of the original is retained but the English version is more exploratory and subjective. The Latin poem never strays far from the sacraments themselves; although the personal note is present it is always controlled, nearly subdued in the contemplation of the sacramental objects and the "latens deitas" (concealed God). From the opening lines, Crashaw's speaker is more intensely and more personally involved in his poetic quest for faith, and the result is more animated, more energetic, but thus less contemplative and assured:

> With all the powres my poor Heart hath
> Of humble love and loyall Faith,
> Thus lowe (my hidden life!) I bow to thee
> Whom too much love hath bow'd more low for me.
> Down down, proud sense! Discourses dy.
> Keep close, my soul's inquiring ey! (1–6)

The Latin addresses the bread of the memorial rite in a prayer for life and sweet taste: "O memoriale mortis domini,/Panis vivus, vitam praestans homini:/Praesta meæ menti de te vivere/Et te illi semper dulce sapere." Crashaw's comparable lines are richer in imagery and more enthusiastic and subjective in tone:

> O dear memoriall of that Death
> Which lives still, and allowes us breath!
> Rich, Royall food! Bountyfull BREAD!
> Whose use denyes us to the dead;

> Whose vitall gust alone can give
> The same leave both to eat and live;
> Live ever Bread of loves, and be
> My life, my soul, my surer selfe to mee. (37–44)

A small but dramatic difference between the Latin and Crashaw's version typifies the different aims and effects of the two poems. St. Thomas maintains throughout a personal tone that invites, at the same time, the participation of an audience. Thus the medieval hymn carefully balances the personal and the universal, viewing the individual response in a ritual, and thus more public, medium. This balance is reflected structurally and thematically in the penultimate stanza. Jesus, the life-giving pelican, can save the single sinner with His blood; one drop can, indeed, save the whole world from its sins: "Pie pellicane, Jesu domine,/Me immundum munda tuo sanguine/Cujus una stilla salvum facere/Totum mundum quit ab omni scelere." In Crashaw there is no more than a glance at other sinners; the world that can be saved by one drop of Christ's blood has been transformed into the "worlds of sins" of the poet himself:

> O soft self-wounding Pelican!
> Whose brest weepes Balm for wounded man.
> Ah this way bend thy benign floud
> To'a bleeding Heart that gaspes for blood.
> That blood, whose least drops soveraign be
> To wash my worlds of sins from me.
> Come love! Come LORD! and that long day
> For which I languish, come away. (45–52)

In Crashaw's version the ritual quality thus yields to the more personal and introspective petition of the speaker.

Even closer to the original poetry of St. Thomas is Crashaw's rendering of the sequence for the feast of Corpus Christi, "Lauda Sion Salvatorem." While Crashaw's version of the "Adoro Te" augments the pattern of the original and embellishes it considerably, his paraphrase of the sequence of the mass emulates the progressive development of the original and matches its eighty-line length. Those characteristics we associate with the later Crashaw—a more florid rhetoric, a more exclamatory tone—are not absent in this poem but they are less conspicuous than in his other hymns.

"Lauda Sion Salvatorem," so intimately tied to the celebration of the mass, is a thorough response to the occasion and meaning of the sacramental feast. Sion is urged to praise its savior and shepherd, although he is beyond praise, because he has appointed the living and life-giving bread ("Panis vivus et vitalis") to be taken as a memorial of the holy supper given to the twelve apostles. The new law manifested in the memorial mass does away with the old law; as Crashaw phrases it, "a new Lamb blesses the Board" while "the aged Pascha . . . spyes love's dawn, and disappeares." The crux of the celebration rite is found in the last half of each poem, as the poet looks with a closer eye at the sacramental objects and the transmutation they undergo. Crashaw's sixth and seventh stanzas follow St. Thomas's originals closely, underscoring both the "unnatural" changes that occur during the celebration of the supper and the faith necessary to accept such a mystery:

> The Heavn-instructed house of FAITH
> Here a holy Dictate hath
> That they but lend their Form and face,
> Themselves with reverence leave their place
> Nature, and name, to be made good
> By'a nobler Bread, more needfull BLOOD.

> Where nature's lawes no leave will give,
> Bold FAITH takes heart, and dares beleive.
> In different species, names not things
> Himself to me my SAVIOUR brings,
> As meat in That, as Drink in this;
> But still in Both one CHRIST he is. (31–42)

The remainder of the sequence underscores the integrity and efficacy of the sacraments and the continuing nourishment received from Christ; although the bread may be broken, each communicant receives the "whole CHRIST in every crumme." Thus this bread of angels ("panis angelorum") feeds men and is the archetypal offering prefigured by three events out of the old law— the near offering of Isaac, the manna given to the Israelites, and the ritual offering of the paschal lamb. The sequence then closes with a prayer to Jesus as good shepherd and true bread ("Bone pastor, panis vere") that this memorial feast anticipate a fuller celebration in heaven.

Sister Margaret Claydon observes that Crashaw's version contains some representative changes but to a lesser degree—an increase of adjectives, more exclamatory utterances, more person-ification.[11] Even more significant is Crashaw's greater emphasis on the role of love in the commemorative feast. St. Thomas's original gives priority to faith; Crashaw notes the requisite faith but speaks to the powerful motivation of love as well. It is love that prompts the praise of Sion in the first stanza just as it is love that lies behind the sacrifice that allows the memorial (stanza two). Crashaw's paraphrase of stanza three, although remarkably true to the order, theme, and even, at times, the language of the original, nonetheless is more personal and emotive and invites love to be cocelebrant:

> Come, love! and let us work a song
> Lowd and pleasant, sweet and long;
> Let lippes and Hearts lift high the noise
> Of so just and solemn joyes,
> Which on his white browes this bright day
> Shall hence for ever bear away. (13–18)

As attention to the prime motivation of love begins Crashaw's poem, so it ends it as well. Crashaw first describes a love that was the motive for Christ's sacrifice and for the response of His followers; the final stanza reinforces this reciprocal relationship through the agency of love:

> O let that love which thus makes thee
> Mix with our low Mortality,
> Lift our lean Soules, and sett us up
> Convictors of thine own full cup,
> Coheirs of SAINTS. (73–77)

"Dies Iræ Dies Illa," a seventeen-stanza poem in rhymed tercets, is traditionally viewed as the most impressive of the medieval hymns, the solemn and awe-inspiring masterpiece of the genre.[12] Written by Thomas of Celano, the original was used as the sequence for the Requiem Mass and thus contemplates, with a combination of dread and cautious hope, the final day of wrath ("dies iræ"). The poem contains two parts, one more descriptive and objective, the other more personal and emotional. The first six tercets, just over a third of the poem, describe the day of wrath, the destruction of the world, the coming of the Judge to decide the fate of humankind. The remaining eleven stanzas are more personal as the speaker contemplates his own soul on that final day: "Quid sum miser tunc dicturus?" (Then what will I say in my wretchedness?). The speaker urges forgiveness and mercy, but the tone remains cautious and tormented throughout; the position of the speaker is reinforced in the final lines, as he speaks with supplication and humility and pleads for the care of God: "Oro supplex et acclinis,[13]/Cor contritum, quasi cinis:/Gere curam mei finis."

As with the two poems of the other Thomas, Crashaw in his version follows fairly closely the progression of images and themes of the original. There is some attempt to reflect the two parts and two moods of the original, but Crashaw's poem blurs the division and the balance by introducing the personal element even in the first lines: "Hears't thou, my soul, what serious things/Both the Psalm and sybyll sings/Of a sure judge" (1-3). The trumpetal solemnity of the original is diminished further by Crashaw's more excited and more evocative rhetoric. The impact of the Latin is at times enhanced through the cold, frightful portrait of that awful time: "Mors stupebit et natura,/Cum resurget creatura,/Judicanti responsura." Crashaw's depiction of the same moment sacrifices solemnity for excitement:

> Horror of nature, hell and Death!
> When a deep Groan from beneath
> Shall cry we come, we come and all
> The caves of night answer one call. (13-16)

The second part of Crashaw's poem stresses further the personal note of concern and distress and almost always with greater emotion than in the original. Thomas pleads with the king of terrible majesty, who grants grace to all who would be saved, to save as a fountain of pity ("Rex tremendæ majestatis,/Qui salvandos salvas gratis,/Salva me fons pietatis"). Crashaw seeks more luxurious assurance and comfort:

> But thou giv'st leave (dread Lord) that we
> · Take shelter from thy self, in thee;
> And with the wings of thine own dove
> Fly to thy scepter of soft love. (25-28)

Christ the Judge is present in the poem, but He is also addressed as

"Dear" and as "my Freind." Crashaw is not comfortable with the images of dread and power evoked so consistently in "Dies Iræ," and he therefore balances those images with images and emotions of a different sort not found or not emphasized in the original: "The wings of thine own dove," "thy scepter of soft love," the speaker's "blushing Cheek and bleeding ey." In brief, Crashaw's Lord is characterized less by his unyielding judgment than by his "bounteous self" which offers hope for this "suppliant heart."

The final three paraphrases reflect most of the stylistic and tonal changes discussed previously, but they demonstrate even greater freedom from the Latin and, particularly in "O Gloriosa Domina," considerable expansion beyond the lines and aims of the originals.

"Vexilla Regis" was a hymn to be sung at Vespers during Passiontide and during the feast of the Holy Cross.[14] The Latin gives balanced attention to the cross and the crucified, beginning and ending with an evocative portrait of the mystery of the cross ("crucis mysterium") that encloses, in the structure of the poem, a portrait of the victim. The result is fairly graphic attention to the crucifixion scene and a fairly literal rendering of the details of the event. The cross is praised because it has been favored with the body of Christ and because it provides the only hope ("spes unica") for those who witness to the mystery of the climax of the Incarnation.

From the opening line Crashaw turns the ritual statement into a more personal exclamation of his own anguish and the efficacy of love:

> Look up, languishing Soul! Lo where the fair
> BADG of thy faith calls back thy care,
>   And biddes thee ne're forget
>   Thy life is one long Debt
> Of love to Him, who on this painfull TREE
> Paid back the flesh he took for thee. (1–6)

As we saw in "Lauda Sion Salvatorem" Crashaw views love as both ascending and descending, directed up toward Christ because of the love manifested downward in the Incarnation:

> Lo, how the streames of life, from that full nest
> Of loves, thy lord's too liberall brest,
>   Flow in an amorous floud
>   Of WATER wedding BLOOD. (7–10)

The water/blood image is found in the original but there it is more pictorial and doctrinal; water mixes with blood after the spear wound to wash away sins ("Ut nos lavaret crimine/Manavit unda sanguine"). Crashaw enriches the imagery by evoking far-reaching effects and emotions; "the streames of life . . . Flow in an amorous floud," having been prompted by the "full nest/Of loves." Later we read of the "great LOVE" that leads to the "wounds of love" suffered on the cross; the cross itself is a "Larg throne of love!" and it is specifically love—in Crashaw's poem but not in the original— that, manifested in the sacrifice of Christ, outweighs the threat of death. Throughout Crashaw's version, imagery is more vivid, emotion is more acutely felt, the personal note is more often struck. It may be too much to claim, with Claydon, that Crashaw's is a "completely new poem," but it is clearly a very different one.[15]

If "Dies Iræ Dies Illa" is the solemn masterpiece of the medieval hymns, the most intimate and tender is the "Stabat Mater Dolorosa," the hymn on the sorrows of the Virgin contemplating her crucified Son. The author was probably Jacopone da Todi, and the hymn was used as the sequence for the Feast in Passiontide and on September 15; it later had more varied uses at Vespers, Matins, and Lauds.[16] The Latin poem, composed of thirteen stanzas of six lines each, opens with a portrait of the crucifixion scene as described in John.[17] The mother of sorrows stands near the cross weeping and sharing the suffering of her Son. The irony of the "blessed" virgin now so sorrowful is not lost on the poet; "benedicta" turns to "afflicta" and sets the tone for the remainder of the poem. The poet responds to the mother as mourner and also, though less, to the Son as victim. He prays for the pain of her mourning that he may willingly join her in sorrow ("Te libenter sociare,/Cum planctu desidero"). By mourning with her he will also be wounded by the wounds of her Son ("Fac me plagis vulnerari") and participate in his passion. The poem closes with a prayer to the Virgin to be his defense and intercessor in the day of judgment.

Da Todi's poem contains the germ of a number of motifs and images expanded and accentuated in Crashaw's translation, "Sancta Maria Dolorum": the tears of sorrow and, alternately, tears of love, the stigmatalike wounding by the wounds of Christ, the simultaneous experiences of pain felt by both mother and Son and requested by the poet, the inebriation resulting from contemplation of the cross and blood ("Cruce fac inebriari/Et cruore filii").

Furthermore, its style, though simpler than Crashaw's exuberant English version, is, as Warren notes, "already rhetorically and musically rich."[18] The "Stabat Mater," though aptly characterized as a "Plainsong" in the heading, is, in fact, much less plain than the other hymns Crashaw translated.

Reading Crashaw's poem, we are struck most of all by the intricate and developing relationship existing between the sorrowful mother, the suffering Christ, and the sympathetic poet, and the extension of the poem beyond the localized scene of the crucifixion into the heart and emotions of the speaker. This reciprocity of feelings and wounds is only hinted at in the Latin; that poem focuses almost exclusively on Mary and her sorrows, and when the poet prays to be able to share her sorrows the dominant image remains that of the crucifixion scene itself. The poet will be near her by the cross to share her grief: "Juxta crucem tecum stare,/Te libenter sociare,/Cum planctu desidero."

There is in Crashaw's poem "a perpetual and reciprocal movement" that turns images of sorrow and pain at the crucifixion into symbols of Christian love and redemption.[19] As early as the second stanza the reciprocal pain of mother and Son is underscored rhetorically, as "Her eyes bleed TEARES, his wounds weep BLOOD" (20). There, too, the poet hints at his own developing response. The concord of mutual wounding is most explicit in stanza three, where wounds and deaths are equally shared, not, as in the original, perceived mainly in the observing mother:

> O costly intercourse
> Of deaths, and worse,
> Divided loves. While son and mother
> Discourse alternate wounds to one another;
> Quick Deaths that grow
> And gather, as they come and goe:
> His Nailes write swords in her, which soon her heart
> Payes back, with more than their own smart;
> Her SWORDS, still growing with his pain,
> Turn SPEARES, and straight come home again. (21–30)

The poet's request for his own participation in the reciprocity of wounds and loves is excited and determined and neatly balances the soft warmth of the Virgin and the coldness of his heart:

> O Mother turtle-dove!
> Soft sourse of love
> That these dry lidds might borrow
> Somthing from thy full Seas of sorrow!
> O in that brest
> Of thine (the noblest nest
> Both of love's fires and flouds) might I recline
> This hard, cold, Heart of mine!
> The chill lump would relent, and prove
> Soft subject for the seige of love. (41–50)

In other hymns and poems Crashaw effectively portrays the reciprocal nature of Christian love; here it is especially rich and complex. Love is manifested in the sorrowful mother and the wounded Son and is imaged as darting back and forth between the two; planted imaginatively near the mother the poet may also be struck by the darts of divine love, may

> At least be in loves way;
> And in these chast warres while the wing'd wounds flee
> So fast 'twixt him and thee,
> My brest may catch the kisse of some kind dart,
> Though as at second hand, from either heart. (66–70)

The climax of emotion and reciprocity is stanza eight, where the poet's desire to be overwhelmed by the imaginative scene before him is the unifying force behind tone, rhetoric, and theme:

> O you, your own best Darts
> Dear, dolefull hearts!
> Hail; and strike home and make me see
> That wounded bosomes their own weapons be.
> Come wounds! come darts!
> Nail'd hands! and pierced hearts!
> Come your whole selves, sorrow's great son and mother!
> Nor grudge a yonger-Brother
> Of greifes his portion, who (had all their due)
> One single wound should not have left for you. (71–80)

"Sancta Maria Dolorum" is the richest and most satisfying of the paraphrases, in part, I suspect, because the original already nourishes those qualities Crashaw so consistently creates and enhances in the hymns.[20] The Baroque exuberance and emotional intimacy, which created a discordant note in the "Dies Iræ," is here appropriate for the subject and occasion of the poem. The "Sancta Maria Dolorum" is, along with the Teresa poems, one of Crashaw's best pieces celebrating the power of love to lead to a participation and intoxication with the divine.

Crashaw's other poem on Mary, "O Gloriosa Domina," is based on a portion of a hymn by Fortunatus that was commonly accepted to be sung at Lauds during the Feasts for the Virgin.[21] It is the shortest of the translations (forty lines) but also reflects the greatest expansion upon the original. The relevant portion from Fortunatus's poem contains twelve lines, to which is added a closing doxology. The Latin poem praises Mary as the mother of the one who created her and who brings hope to the world. Mary restores what Eve had lost and is thus the royal door ("regis . . . janua") from which Christ enters the world and the window ("fenestra") through which Eve's children may be allowed to enter heaven. Crashaw's translation is primarily an expansion of the central themes and images of the original. It is less exuberant than the other paraphrases, but reveals Crashaw's equally characteristic fascination with the mysteries of the Incarnation. His poem is a presentation of the mysteries and paradoxes of that seminal event as seen in the person of Mary. She is portrayed as "Above the world" but "below thy SON" (2); the maker of all things made himself her Son; varying the metaphor, the "FEAST of all things feeds on thee" (10). Eve, the first "mother," brought death to all while she herself was still childless; Mary's "healthfull womb" has "given us heav'n again, in giving HIM" (20), and she is thus more appropriately called the "mother" of the world. Crashaw's principal attention is given to the image of Mary as door or window, introduced concisely in six lines of the Latin poem but repeated and explored in a kind of oscillating movement in nineteen lines of Crashaw's version. Mary's womb is the "world's new eastern window" that emits a "Rosy DAWN" and creates day out of Eve's night. The paradox of the Virgin birth is imposed on the door imagery drawn from the original poem: Mary is the "door of life: and sourse of day!" through which "LIGHT was seen and LIFE reveald." Yet, since Mary was a virgin, the door was shut: "The door was shutt, yet let in day,/The fountain seald, yet life found way" (35–36).

"O Gloriosa Domina" is a poem whose subject was surely a favorite one of Crashaw, yet in tone and emotional rhetoric it is relatively subdued. Or, more accurately, the emotional peaks are matched by an analytical perception of the mystery of Mary's role as the mother of Christ and the world; the result is a poem where praise and joy are firmly under control.

II The Hymns

Among the original hymns composed by Crashaw, "In the Glorious Assumption of Our Blessed Lady. A Hymn" presents further evidence of Crashaw's enthusiasm for the subject of Mary and the images and emotions associated with her: hearts and love, a "rosy princesse" and a "holy Queen," the comfort and warmth of maternity and the hope of immortality. The Hymn in the Assumption follows "O Gloriosa Domina" in *Carmen Deo Nostro*, and the two poems taken together form a fitting and adoring tribute to the mother of Jesus, from Incarnation to Assumption.

The Assumption Hymn is separated from the remaining four devotional hymns in subject and doctrine though not in style.[22] The hymns to the Name of Jesus, in the Holy Nativity, for New Year's Day, and in the Glorious Epiphanie celebrate the name and Incarnation of Jesus, invoking the perpetual appearance and incarnation of Jesus in the first poem and recalling the historical Incarnation in the remaining three. The Hymn in the Assumption alone celebrates the mother of Jesus, now ascended into heaven to rejoin Christ, "the dear immortall dove."

The poem first appeared in the 1646 *Steps* and then in an altered version in 1648 and 1652. The second version is more successful and is a more interesting poem. Its principal changes are the addition of ten lines (17–26) that divide and amplify lines taken from the Song of Songs, and the deletion of ten lines (31–40 in the original) that disrupt the immediate impact of the hymn.

Crashaw's poem reveals the imagery and style of the source from which it received the lines that are explored through rhetorical amplification:

> Rise up, my fair, my spotlesse one!
> The winter's past, the rain is gone.
> The spring is come, the flowrs appear
> No sweets, but thou, are wanting here. (9–12)[23]

Christ appears in this poem as he was interpreted typologically to appear in the Song of Songs, as the bridegroom and lover, calling his spouse to unite with him. The Assumption is thus not so much a departure from earth as an inevitable return and reunion: "heavn must goe home." The first forty-three lines of the poem offer two dominant motifs: in her assumption into heaven Mary reveals her superiority over natural creatures and objects, and in that assumption she is following the bidding of love.

Mary is a "peice of heav'nly earth; Purer and brighter/Then the chast starres" (3-4). Nature acts in accordance with her action, serving as a mute chorus celebrating her imminent transcendence. More evocative are the lines of love, repeated later in the poem and serving as a ritual call of the bridegroom to his mate:

> Come away, my love!
> Come away, my dove! cast off delay,
> The court of heav'n is come
> To wait upon thee home; Come come away! (13-16)

Lines 44-69 are the hymn proper, sung in celebration of the Assumption and the "pretious name." The song serves a double purpose, however. It praises the Virgin and thereby pays her appropriate tribute. But in the invoking of her name she is kept alive and present in her adorers, thus challenging the claims of the Assumption itself:

> Thy pretious name shall be
> Thy self to us; and we
> With holy care will keep it by us.
> We to the last
> Will hold it fast
> And no ASSUMPTION shall deny us. (46-51)

The efficacy and variety of Mary's roles are implied in the titles she is given in the hymn: she is the "holy Queen of humble hearts," the "mother of our KING," the "rosy princesse," and the "Queen of men." Her power to inspire in Crashaw his fondest images and emotions is evident throughout the poem, and nowhere more than at the end. A litany of names for the Virgin reveals the comfort given to, and by, the new mother of humankind:

O may the best
Of everlasting joyes bath thy white brest.
LIVE, our chast love, the holy mirth
Of heavn; the humble pride of earth.
Live, crown of woemen; Queen of men.
Live mistresse of our song. And when
Our weak desires have done their best,
Sweet Angels come, and sing the rest. (62–69)

The first poem of the *Carmen Deo Nostro* is the poem to the
Countess of Denbigh, serving as a kind of dedicatory offering to
the woman to whom the volume is formally presented. Following
that poem, and thus gaining both textual and thematic primacy, are
the four major hymns on Jesus and the Incarnation. The first
establishes the dominant tone and subject to which each of the
poems gives attention, for it is essentially "the name above every
name, the name of Jesus" that the poems individually and in unison
celebrate.

The Hymn to the Name of Jesus was likely composed for the
Feast of the Holy Name, celebrated between Circumcision and
Epiphany and thus additionally tied to the events of the Incarnation.[24] If the origin of Crashaw's poem is the medieval *Jubilus de
nomine Jesu*, as Praz suggests, the indebtedness is slight at best.[25]
Crashaw may have gotten from the *Jubilus* its attentiveness to the
senses, and some of the dominant motifs of the seventeenth-
century poem do indeed remind the reader of several lines and
images of the medieval hymn. Sweet is the memory of Jesus ("Jesu
dulcis memoria"), the medieval poet proclaims, but sweet above
honey and all else is His presence ("Sed super mel et omnia/Ejus
dulcis præsentia"). Jesus is sweet music to the ears ("aure dulce
canticum"), an object for men to taste, and a light ("lumine")
shining in a world of darkness. Beyond such possible, and slight,
influences, the hymns exist as two poems celebrating the same
subject but in dramatically different ways.

Louis Martz's analysis of the structure and development of the
Hymn to the Name of Jesus remains largely beyond dispute. He
demonstrates that, as "one of the great achievements in the poetry
of meditation," Crashaw's poem follows the *Scala Meditatoria* of
Mauburnus (and its English manifestation in Joseph Hall's *The
Arte of Divine Meditation* [1606]) and proceeds through seven
divisions: I (1–12) "Introduction: proposal of the subject and

introductory prayer"; II (13–45) "Preliminary self-address"; III
(46–87) "Address to all creatures, asking for their assistance"; IV
(88–114) "Self-address, justifying the speaker's own place in the
celebration"; V (115–50) "Invocation of the Name, calling for its
appearance; first part of the 'hymn,' proper"; VI (151–96) "Celebration of the appearance of the Name: second part of the 'hymn,'
proper"; and VII (197–239) "Conclusion: the faith of the ancient
martyrs contrasted with the lack of faith at the present moment of
history."[26] As Martz's notes indicate, the present hymn, like those
that follow it in the *Carmen Deo Nostro*, celebrates an Incarnation
experience, not, in this instance, the historical one but the
continuing one, a kind of lasting "Epiphany" realized by those who
participate in the celebrative rites.[27]

The poem begins in an epiclike strain and pronounces the sacred
nature of its subject: "I sing the NAME which None can say/But
touch't with An interiour RAY." The inner light by which this name
is celebrated is, however, acknowledged in the poem through an
overt appeal to the senses. The awakening of the soul to the
celebration of the Name (line 13) is also an awakening to full
participation in sensuous analogies, and the divisions of the poem
correspond, not only to stages of the scale of meditation, but also to
several of the individual senses. Thus, as Wallerstein notes, it "is the
senses, organized and enlarged by a great art, which the poet calls
upon to lift him from out the dull world of daily perception. It is the
concept of Christ which must translate the senses themselves."[28]

Each of three divisions of the poem is dominated by particular
sense experiences, each emphasis appropriate for that stage of the
celebrative experience. Having aroused his soul, the poet urges
"Great NATURE" and all created things to join in the song and
therefore invites us to hear the "Fitt-tun'd Harmony" (section III).
Assured of his own proper place in this chorus (IV), the poet can
then proceed to the hymn proper, beginning first with an
invocation to the "lovely Name" to appear and thus appealing to
our sight (V), and advancing from there to the appearance of the
Name, characterized by sweetness and balm and stimulating both
taste and smell (VI).

Section III urges the awakening of "LUTE and HARP/And
every sweet-lipp't Thing/That talkes with tunefull string" to join in
the "Fitt-tun'd Harmony" (46–50). The controlling metaphor of
this section is underscored in lines 56–58, as music becomes a

definition of existence itself: "All Things that Are,/Or, what's the same,/Are Musicall." The poet seeks help from the "soft ministers of sweet sad mirth" as he "meditate[s] mine Immortall Song." Nature joins with art in the "conspiracy of our Spatious song"; the "Powres of Praise" produce a "common mirthe" from "Vessells of vocall Joyes." The section ends by moving from the heard music of earthly praise, to the unheard music of the "noble Architects of Intellectuall Noise," the song of the heavens that falls on souls, not ears. There is, finally, through the powerful stimulus of love, a mingling of all praising beings in an eternal song of joy: "O may you fix/For ever here, and mix/Your selves into the long/And everlasting series of a deathlesse SONG" (82–85).

The praise of the Name is thus presented in an analogy that invites singing and hearing, the harmony and fitness of the object of praise mirrored in the "musical ecstasy" of the song.[29] The appearance of the Name is anticipated by the eyes of the mind, made analogous to the physical sight of those who, having sung, now see. In section V the "lovely NAME" is called to "Appeare from forth the Bright/Regions of peacefull Light," to be "The gracious Guest/Of humble Soules, that seek to find/The hidden Sweets/Which man's heart meets/When Thou art Master of the Mind" (115–24). The Name is master of the heart, the soul, the mind, but the way to the inner light is, in this Baroque poem, through the analogy to physical sight. "The'attending WORLD, to wait thy Rise,/First turn'd to eyes," and the eyes then turn to tears. The hopefulness of the celebrants is contrasted with the anguish derived from the absence of the object celebrated, and the whole of the image is located within the governing metaphor of seeing:

> O come away
> And kill the DEATH of This Delay.
> O see, so many WORLDS of barren yeares
> Melted and measur'd out in Seas of TEARES.
> O see, The WEARY liddes of wakefull Hope
> (LOVE'S Eastern windowes) All wide ope
> With Curtains drawn,
> To catch The Day-break of Thy DAWN. (141–48)

The actual coming of the Name (section VI) is imaged in lines suggesting the immediacy and intimacy of the experience. The way to a religious perception of the sweetness of the Name of Jesus

is through a sensuous apprehension of fragrance and taste. From
the Name "SWEETES are suck't"; it is the Hive "Where All [the]
Hoard of Hony lyes." The Name, manifesting the sweet odors of
sanctity, disperses its "spicy Powres" in "balmy showrs." The poet
wishes for a fullness of the experience, to be totally consumed by
the sweetness of the Name to the obliteration of all profane
concerns: "O fill our senses, And take from us/All force of so
Prophane a Fallacy/To think ought sweet but that which smells of
Thee" (170–72). As so often happens in the Baroque experience,
the physical senses are evoked finally to be overwhelmed by the
higher perception of divinity; the only lasting sweetness is not
physical, but "that which smells of Thee." The dominant analogy
continues, however, as we are led to experience the "Nectareall
Fragrancy," the "universal SYNOD of All sweets," the "Perfume"
and "Frankincense" and "Mountains of myrrh"—in sum, the "ten
Thousand PARADISES/The soul that tasts thee takes from
thence."

This sensuous consummation devoutly to be wished does not
end the poem but it is clearly the climax of theme and imagery. The
final section is more retrospective in view and tempered in tone;
we are reminded of saints and martyrs whose own witnessing and
deaths made more certain the continual dawning and epiphany of
the Name. Sensuous ecstasy is moderated by recollection and
affirmation. In more controlled rhetoric, although with no less
certain impact, the closing of the poem confirms the final
supremacy of the Name there celebrated:

> They that by Love's mild Dictate now
> Will not adore thee,
> Shall Then with Just Confusion, bow
> And break before thee. (236–39)

The Hymn to the Name of Jesus celebrates the Holy Name and
celebrates as well the sensuous way to God. The fullest evocation
of the senses leads to the fullest awareness of God.

The three poems on the historical Incarnation form a tightly
woven fabric of imagery and color, each part related to the others
but exhibiting its own distinct texture and shading. The Hymn in
the Holy Nativity, the only one of the three to undergo significant
revision by Crashaw, is the first in the chronology of events and in
its location in *Carmen Deo Nostro*. The Nativity Hymn is sung

principally by the shepherds Tityrus and Thyrsis, usually in alternating stanzas but with certain passages in which they join voices and others in which a full chorus sings, notably at the beginning and ending.

Crashaw's changes from the original version of 1646 are almost uniformly effective. The first version compliments the child and the mother in language that is immediately pertinent but limited in its theological or symbolic impact. The second version reinforces the singular and symbolic significance of the event by altering a few words, adding two important stanzas, repeating a stanza important for its attention to symbol and imagery, and eliminating one stanza from 1646 that is thematically discordant.[30]

The Hymn in the Nativity is dominated by two motifs: the act of seeing that leads to a continual recognition of the "blest Sight" and the particular meaning and effects of this appearance. The shepherds speak continually of what they have seen, and their words are thus reminiscent of the similarly blessed sight of the chorus celebrating the Holy Name: through their "blest Sight" the shepherds find out "Heavn's fairer ey" contrasting with an object useful only "to mortall Sight." The eyes of the child Jesus ("those sweet eyes' persuasive powrs") are able to control Nature, and in the only fully repeated stanza the two shepherds together praise the light they have seen:

> We saw thee in thy baulmy Nest,
> Young dawn of our æternall DAY!
> We saw thine eyes break from their EASTE
> And chase the trembling shades away.
> We saw thee; and we blest the sight
> We saw thee by thine own sweet light. (31–36)

Physical sight of the child, important as it is, is transcended by the sight that yields understanding, and the shepherds therefore testify to the meaning of the Nativity for the world. The child shows himself superior to Nature in the controlling images of the poem, taking precedence over the light of the sun, bringing day into the nighttime of his birth, subduing the harsh effects of winter and turning frost to flowers. Symbols spring from images, as the physical and historical events begin to take place not in time but in eternity. The babe is the "Young dawn of our æternall DAY," and he transcends the ordinary limitations of his birth. The two stanzas added by Crashaw emphasize this dimension of the event as do no other parts of the original version:

> Tity. Poor WORLD (said I.) what wilt thou doe
>   To entertain this starry STRANGER?
> Is this the best thou canst bestow?
>   A cold, and not too cleanly, manger?
> Contend, ye powres of heav'n and earth.
> To fitt a bed for this huge birthe. (37–42)

> Thyr. Proud world, said I; cease your contest
>   And let the MIGHTY BABE alone.
> The Phænix builds the Phænix' nest.
>   LOVE'S architecture is his own.
> The BABE whose birth embraves this morn,
> Made his own bed e're he was born. (44–49)

We see in the final version of the poem, but not in the original, a pattern alternating between the immediate scene of the Nativity and explicit reminders of what that event truly means. From the stanzas quoted above the poem moves to three that focus more on the Nativity scene itself, although we are reminded of the presence of the Seraphims and of the fact that "HEAVN itself lyes here below." Following these stanzas is the repeated stanza, stressing the measure, not of time, but of the "æternall Day."

The closing five stanzas, spoken as a triumphant welcome by the full chorus, is similarly structured. The middle three stanzas are more exactly focused on the immediate and historical scene, moving from the Virgin Mother, to the shepherds themselves, and to their gifts from nature. The first and last stanzas of the five serve largely to recall the dramatic paradoxes and the simultaneous changing of roles implicit in the event. The first captures the wondrous mysteries inherent in the appearance of the child:

> Wellcome, all WONDERS in one sight!
>   ÆEternity shutt in a span.
> Sommer in Winter. Day in Night.
>   Heaven in earth, and GOD in MAN.
> Great little one! whose all-embracing birth
> Lifts earth to heaven, stoopes heav'n to earth. (79–84)

The last stanza anticipates the response of those who serve the child king, a response itself characterized by a kind of wonder:

To THEE, meek Majesty! soft KING
Of simple GRACES and sweet LOVES.
Each of us his lamb will bring
Each his pair of sylver Doves;
Till burnt at last in fire of Thy fair eyes,
Our selves become our own best SACRIFICE. (103–108)

The shortest and thematically the most modest of the hymns is the Hymn on the Circumcision or "New Year's Day." The Circumcision Hymn picks up from the previous poems the theme of the superiority of the supernatural Son over the natural sun, colors the occasion of the poem with brilliant reds and purples, and looks forward to the more profound treatment of the Son and the sun in the Epiphany Hymn.

The Nativity Hymn advances from physical sight to understanding and contemplation; the Circumcision Hymn uses sight and color largely for their immediate and sensuous effect. The morning of the day commemorated is "Rosy with a double Red" since it has both the "blush" of its dawn and the "dear drops" of blood from the circumcision. The "purple pride" and "red-ey'd Rubies" of nature and the dawn, symbolic of their worth, are as nothing compared to the rich color emanating from the child. When the sun has done all it can "To make himselfe rich in his rise,/All will be darknes to the Day/That breakes from one of these bright eyes" (26–28). The dominating imagery of reds, suggestive of the dawn and the blood of the circumcision, gives way in the last four stanzas to a more explicit contrast between light and dark, day and night, and in that development the poem most obviously anticipates the focus of the Epiphany Hymn.[31] The sun, to this point an object of potential power and beauty, is further portrayed in the final stanzas as a god, but one whose worshippers will forsake him for the child. Power, beauty, and deity are thus denied the sun because of the coming of the child. The "seeing" that defines the response of the choruses of worshipers in the first two hymns is matched by the light that shines forth from the eyes of the child, "bright eyes" from which darkness turns to day, "fairest eyes" that give the world not one sun but two.

The Hymn in the Glorious Epiphanie is the thematic and theological climax of the four poems, but it reveals, as well, a remarkably different approach to the central concern of each of the poems: the realization of God through the poetic celebration of His Incarnation. The luxury of the earlier hymns is largely kept out in the Epiphany Hymn, as rosy and purple colors give way to the starkness of light and dark and as the worship of God through the senses yields to the achievement of the "frugall negative light," the *via negativa* to God. Warren suggests that the relationship between the Epiphany Hymn and the Nativity Hymn

is one to invite speculation. The latter contemplates the Child Jesus sleeping between the pure yet warm breasts of His Mother; the former contemplates the God of the philosophers, the Logos, the *Lumen de Lumine*. . . . Of the two types of mystics, the visionaries and the philosophers, Crashaw's temperament markedly allied him with the former; and the *via negativa*, with its denial of sensuous analogies, runs counter to the baroque belief that in my flesh shall I see God in His flesh.[32]

The most important association is not, however, with the Nativity Hymn but with the Hymn to the Name of Jesus. The first poem of these four invites the fullest sensuous apprehension of God, and the imagery is accordingly lush and evocative. The last poem of the four teaches a way to God by achieving an inner light quite apart from, indeed, quite conflicting with, sensuous ecstasy. Other poems remind us that for Crashaw the God of Love was best approached through sensuous analogies, but the Epiphany Hymn is a notable example of a different way.

The Epiphany Hymn is a long exploration of the contrast between the sun and the Son, the apparent brightness of the one darkened by the metaphysical brightness of the other. The paradox is enhanced by the roles of the singers of the poem, the three kings of the Orient. They are sun-worshipers from the East who have come westward to find their true sun in the brightness of the child: "To THEE, thou DAY of night! thou east of west!/Lo we at last have found the way./To thee, the world's great universal east./The Generall and indifferent DAY" (22–25). The present darkening of the sun by the appearance of the greater light and by the rejection of its former worshipers anticipates the profound darkening of the sun at the Crucifixion, and the Epiphany Hymn thus joins two of the central events of Christian history, the Incarnation and the Crucifixion:

> Time has a day in store
> When this so proudly poor
> And self-oppressed spark, that has so long
> By the love-sick world bin made

> Not so much their sun as SHADE,
> Weary of this Glorious wrong
> From them and from himself shall flee
> For shelter to the shadow of thy TREE. (133–40)

The eclipse of the sun is seen as a kind of penitence performed in order to repay the worship that the sun, the "fair-ey'd fallacy of day," has falsely received. The irony of the source of light turned to darkness is heightened when the singers prophesy that it will be the sun's eclipsed darkness, not its awesome light, that will lead false worshipers to the "true LIGHT": "And their best use of him they worship't be/To learn of Him at lest, to worship Thee" (181–82). One such convert was Dionysius the Areopagite, a pagan sun-worshiper who, witnessing the eclipse, gave himself to Christianity. Crashaw describes the transformation in the sun and the worshiper in his poem:

> By the oblique ambush of this close night
> Couch't in that conscious shade
> The right-ey'd Areopagite
> Shall with a vigorous guesse invade
> And catche thy quick reflex; and sharply see
> On this dark Ground
> To descant THEE. (189–95)

The final fifty lines are in many ways the most remarkable of the poem, both because of their effective and concise iteration of dominant themes and images and because of their contrast with the other hymns. The Areopagite proposed the *via negativa*, the negative way to God. Through emptying, not filling, the senses, mystical ascent to God could be accomplished. Dionysius's description of the "negative way" is found in his *The Mystical Theology*, and he there urges the achievement of the realm beyond light, the understanding and union that leave the senses and intellect behind:

Guide us to that topmost height of mystic lore which exceedeth light and more than exceedeth knowledge, where the simple, absolute, and unchangeable mysteries of heavenly Truth lie hidden in the dazzling obscurity of the secret Silence, outshining all brilliance with the intensity of their darkness, and surcharging our blinded intellects with the utterly impalpable and invisible fairness of glories which exceed all beauty! . . . I counsel that . . . thou leave the senses and the activities of the intellect and all things that the senses or the intellect can perceive, and all things in this world of nothingness, or in that world of being, and that, thine understanding being laid to rest, thou strain . . . towards an union with Him whom neither being nor understanding can contain. For, by the unceasing and absolute renunciation of thyself and all things, thou shalt in pureness cast all things aside, and be released from all, and so shalt be led upwards to the Ray of that divine Darkness which exceedeth all existence.[33]

Crashaw speaks similarly, though much more briefly, of the mystic who will

> teach obscure MANKIND a more close way
> By the frugall negative light
> Of a most wise and well-abused Night
> To read more legible thine originall Ray,
> And make our Darknes serve THY day. (208–12)

In this poem imagery oscillates between the "confederat BLACK and WHITE," making simple associations impossible. The natural source of light, the sun, is darkened by the light of a new child, but that darkness leads to an enlightened recognition of the child in the eyes of those who now worship Him. The darkness of the eclipse makes light and understanding available to Dionysius and others, and they will be led further on the ascent to God and his "sparkling Throne" by achieving an inner light, a spiritual seeing, that is an awareness of what Dionysius terms the "secret Silence," the "divine Darkness which exceedeth all existence." The Hymn to the Name of Jesus and the Nativity Hymn speak of an inner revelation by the analogical experience of sight; in contrast, the realization of God in the Epiphany Hymn is achieved by closing the eyes and subduing the senses, not by accentuating them: "Now [we] by abased liddes shall learn to be/Eagles; and shutt our eyes that we may see" (231–32).

The Epiphany Hymn is a notable achievement in its own right and an important poem in the context of Crashaw's sacred canon. It is structurally tight, moving steadily and effectively in time and beyond time, encompassing the historical span of the Incarnation experience from Epiphany through Crucifixion and anticipating the continuing revelation of God to His people through mystical ascent. Imagery of black and white dominates the coloring of the poem, but the complexity and profundity of the associations belie any assumption of simplistic meanings. By the end of the poem, in fact, neither black nor white has any one or two meanings; rather, each is enriched by the shifting and expanding metaphors of the poem and each testifies to the mysteries to which the poem pays respect. Finally, the poem serves as an engaging and final example (for this study) of Crashaw's accomplishment in a style not thought to be "typically" his. Warren overstates the case in claiming that the Epiphany Hymn, more than any other Crashaw poem, "seems metaphysical in style and intent," but it is clearly at variance in imagery and style with the more Baroque pieces that precede it.[34]

CHAPTER 6

The Teresa Poems

I St. Teresa of Avila

IN 1638 Crashaw's friend and spiritual ally Joseph Beaumont spoke eloquently and passionately in a Latin oration of a saint relatively unheard of ("inauditum") by his Cambridge audience. She writes, the audience is told, with a pen bathed with divine dew ("calamus divino rore perfusus"). How sweet, Beaumont exclaims, to expire in her words; how least a death to die in her writings ("O quanta cum suavitate in illius verbis expires! O quam minime mors esset illius scriptis immori!").[1] How early in his life Crashaw knew of Saint Teresa, the saint who inspired Beaumont's rapture, we cannot be sure. Although Beaumont's comments suggest that she is, to most of his 1638 audience, "inauditum," it is entirely possible that Crashaw may have "discovered" her earlier. No single influence on the final development of his religious passion and his artistic sensibility is so important as that of the appealing and enigmatic Spanish saint, Teresa of Avila, and surely any comments he had read or heard about her would have led him to explore her life and works further.

Teresa was born near Avila and was raised in that city.[2] Her family was wealthy but not aristocratic and presumably provided the conveniences and pleasures appropriate to their means. We know little of this early life except for one curious incident, told briefly by Teresa in her autobiography and picked up by Crashaw and others as a vital part of the intriguing and expanding legend of her life. As a young child, Teresa relates, she was devoted to reading the lives of saints and thus became infatuated with the idea of martyrdom. So strong was this response that she determined, at the age of six, to go with her older brother Rodrigo to seek martyrdom among the Moors. "We grew to resolve," she relates,

> that we would goe into *Barbarie*, amongst the *Mores*, and begg, by the way, as we went; that so we might come, by degrees, to loose our lives there, for our Lord. And it seemed, that he, gave us courage enough, for this purpose, even in that tender age of ours, if we could have found anie meanes, to sett it on foot; but our even having of Parents, seemed to be the greatest hindrance, we had.[3]

The youthful impetuousness is, however, forestalled, and Teresa and her brother, denied martyrdom, play instead as religious recluses.

In terms of the slight attention this event receives in the *Vida*, Teresa's youthful thoughts of martyrdom have been greatly overstressed, forming as they do an integral part of the myth that grew up around her. In another sense, however, the event has perhaps received proper attention, for it reveals the child Teresa possessed of the attributes and virtues later to be seen in the action of the reformer: a determined and devoted spirit, doggedly energetic in pursuit of a goal, fascinated by heavenly felicities and earthly means of achieving them, stubbornly resistant to "reasonable" ways but possessing disarming humor and good will.

Those qualities guided her throughout her life (1515–1582) and help explain her phenomenal success as founder and superior of the Discalced Carmelites. Beginning with minimal support and accompanied first by four orphan girls who served as novices, Teresa overcame opposition from authorities and both physical and spiritual obstacles to realize by the time of her death a dramatic reformation of the Carmelite Order.[4] She founded thirty-two convents and monasteries, including one that Crashaw may have visited in Leyden, and she is arguably the single most important influence on Spanish religious life in the sixteenth century. Most striking, perhaps, is her ability to be common and extraordinary at the same time, to work and sweat and worry and then to achieve the heights of mysticism and spiritual ecstasy. She is thus, as Robert Petersson has concluded, "a saint of extraordinary obstinacy and efficiency, a mystic of phenomenal lucidity and intensity, a woman whose energy, humour, and common sense were legendary even while she lived. She was the outstanding provincial genius of the Counter-Reformation."[5]

Regardless of the exact date Crashaw first began to read and react to Teresa, he must have seen that her life and thought spoke importantly to his own. Upon leaving her comfortable home, Teresa faced the burdens of overcoming physical and (she thought) spiritual limitations and of the frequent resistance to her reform efforts. So restrictive was Spain of the Inquisition that Teresa's *Vida*, written at the request of her religious superiors, was nonetheless initially denounced by the Inquisitors. Altered slightly and again presented to the Inquisitors by a Dominican theologian, the *Vida* was approved and supported.[6] Throughout her early life, from the death of her mother when she was thirteen through the initial stages of her reform movement, Teresa faced the twin obstacles of personal doubt and the threat of official opposition and distrust. Seldom lacking in will and courage, Teresa was nonetheless burdened by ill health (on one occasion she was nearly given up for dead) and was frequently obsessed, as seen in her *Vida*, with doubt about her own spiritual vitality.

Crashaw may well have seen in the life of Teresa of Avila someone whose determination and doubt, personal introspection and public awareness, mirrored his own. It is almost certain that he knew of Teresa when his comfortable life at Peterhouse was being threatened. Preachers at the university were being called in and forced to defend their "popish" statements. Within five years after Beaumont's 1638 oration, Crashaw was forced to leave Cambridge for good. Even more certain than these biographical associations are the spiritual and emotional points of contact between Teresa and Crashaw. His poems leave no doubt that in her he saw a saint who could overcome the limits of earthly pain and sorrow and achieve the heights of religious fulfillment. For someone on the pilgrimage of Crashaw the influence was timely and profound.

In all her writings—some seven major books and other lesser ones—Teresa focuses on the religious life, and the works taken together form a kind of massive spiritual autobiography.[7] Furthermore, her *Vida*, the only strict autobiographical account, serves as the most significant and, for Crashaw's poems, the most revealing of her works. The *Vida* gives appropriate attention to biographical facts, but it is less the chronology of her personal life than the achievements of her mystical life with which the *Vida* is most concerned.

In all of her comments on the mystical life and the attainment of "rapts" or visions, Teresa is aware that the experience is at once spiritual and physical, that it is the soul's achievement of divine understanding or unity but it is manifested through physical experiences as well. This inevitable conjunction of the senses and the spirit lies at the heart of the Baroque affirmation of body and soul, as seen in the works of a Bernini or Poussin or Rubens, and as seen most certainly in the Teresa poems of Crashaw.

The possible discomfort felt by a reader who encounters a physical rendering of a spiritual experience is anticipated by the translator of the 1623 and 1642 English versions of the *Vida*, given the English title *The Flaming Hart*. In his preface he remarks on several features of the saint's life, and then addresses the question of the sensuous quality of the visionary experience. Recognizing that the overt corporality of saints' visions may be offensive to some, he argues that "the important busines, in those cases," is that the experience is received from God:

And so, that Servant, consisting both of a Bodie, and a Soule, his Divine Majestie is also gratiously pleased, manie times, to affect both the Bodie, and the Soule, togeather, with a sensible kind of feeling of that grace; Those outward demonstrations (which speake, as it were, to the Bodie) serving cheifly, but to denote, and describe, in that sort, o the whole man, the influences, and imprefections which then are made, and powred out, into the Soule.[8]

The translator here speaks accurately of the physical and spiritual quality of Teresa's visions, her "sensible kind of feeling of that grace," and Teresa herself confirms this extraordinary unity of body and soul.

She describes her earlier experiences of the awareness of God's presence, occasions when she perceived an unusual closeness, what she calls the "evident feeling of the presence of Almightie God . . . that either he was within me, or els I, all engulfed in him."[9] These early experiences, she says, were not Visions but what "they call . . . Mystical Theologie."[10] Each such occasion is marked by a manifestation at once physical and spiritual and thus wholly neither; the sense of God's presence is a "regalo [a gift], which is neither wholy sensuall, nor wholy spiritual; but it is wholy the guift, and blessing of Almightie God."[11]

Teresa's own "Mystical Theologie" involves further distinctions among the various visionary moments experienced by the devotee, and she is quick to argue the superiority of that kind of experience, a "Rapt," which is both spiritual and corporeal and thus excels the less engulfing Union, which is exclusively mental or internal. The

Rapt, she affirms, has a "very great" advantage over Union: Union is experienced always in the "interiour" part, while Rapts are "Visitations of the Soule, which use to be of a higher Straine" and "produce their Effects, not only interiourly, but exteriourly also." Thus she relates (with implicit approval) the levitation of her body and other "exteriour demonstrations" that accompany her own Rapts.[12]

Teresa's most famous vision is recounted in Chapter 29 of the *Vida*, and it is evident from her description that she has experienced it more than once. It is traditionally thought to have occurred for the first time on August 27, 1559, and that date has been, since 1726, one of the feast days of the Carmelite calendar.[13] The Vision of the Transverberation is, as well, the most thorough and compelling statement of the fully sensuous and spiritual nature of Teresa's ecstasy. Painful yet agonizingly joyful, spiritual yet fully involving the senses, Teresa's transverberation stands as one of the landmarks of mystical literature. "It pleased our Blessed Lord," she begins,

that I should have sometimes, this following Vision. I saw an Angell very neer me, towards my left side, and he appeared to me, in a corporeall forme; though yet I am not wont to see anie thing of that kind, but very rarely. For, though Angells be represented often to me, it is yet, without my seeing them, but only according to that other kind of Vision [i.e., an imaginary vision]. . . . But, in this Vision, our Lord was pleased, that I should see this Angell, after this other manner. He was not great; but rather little; yet withall, he was of very much beautie. His face was so inflamed that he appeared to be of those most Superiour Angells, who seem to be, all in a fire; and he well might be of them, whome we call *Seraphins*; but as for me they never tell me their names, or rankes. . . . I saw, that he had a long Dart of gold in his hand; and at the end of the iron below, me thought, there was a little fire; and I conceaved, that he thrust it, some severall times, through my verie Hart, after such a manner, as that it passed the verie inwards, of my Bowells; and when he drew it back, me thought, it carried away, as much, as it had touched within me; and left all that, which remained, wholy inflamed with a great love of Almightie God. The paine of it, was so excessive, that it forced me to utter those groanes; and the suavitie which that extremitie of paine gave, was also so very excessive, that there was no desiring at all, to be ridd of it; nor can the Soule then, receave anie contentment at all, in lesse, then God Almightie himself.

This is no Corporall, but a Spirituall paine; though yet the Bodie doe not faile, to participate some part thereof; yea and that, not a little. And it is such a deare, delightfull kind of entercourse, which passes heer, between the Soule, and Almightie God, as I beseech him of his infinit goodnes, that he will give some touch, or tast of it, to whosoever shall beleive, that I lye. During the time, when I was in this state, . . . [I] contented my self to consume, with burning-up in my paine, which was to be the greatest glorie for me, that this whole world could afford."[14]

Baroque art did not require such explicit justification to effect its decisive conjunction of body and spirit and its accent on the fully sensuous quality of experience. But the life of Teresa, as it was known through legend and as it was revealed by the saint herself, provided extraordinary fruit for the Baroque spirit—as the works of Bernini, Crashaw, and numerous other admirers testify. In her life and visions is manifested a view of the unity of being through the conjunction of flesh and spirit that becomes one of the distinctive features of the Baroque Counter-Reformation spirit. One result of the Council of Trent was a decisive vivifying of religious art; saints were no longer serene and contemplative but were in various stages of emotional expression, from ecstasy to agony, with real wounds, and tears, and blood.[15] A renewed emphasis on the transformation of the Eucharistic symbols, the bread become flesh, the wine blood, adds meaning to the profound conjunction of the physical and spiritual in other realms.

Religious ecstasy, in practice and in art, provided another way by which the glories of the flesh led to the glories of the spirit. Since the ultimate achievement of the Counter-Reformation was aimed at the unity of body and spirit, the Council of Trent "fostered a view of art which aspired to this unity of being. Man in the flesh cannot attain that unity, yet he may experience something close to it, if briefly and imperfectly."[16] Teresa's own ecstatic visions approximate that perfect union, and the heightened sensuousness and artistic ecstasy of Crashaw's Hymn to Saint Teresa and, especially, the final lines of "The Flaming Heart" confirm his attempt to experience, "briefly and imperfectly," a poetic unity of spirit and flesh that mirrors the perfect one unreachable by earthbound humanity. Ecstasy thus becomes, as Émile Mâle has said, "the culmination of Christian life and the supreme effort of art."[17]

II *Crashaw's Teresa Poems*

Crashaw's three poems in honor of St. Teresa are his ultimate achievement in Baroque art and the most consequential examples of his allegiance to the *via affirmativa*, the way to God through expression and feeling. Baroque art and religious ecstasy are mutually reinforcing, and in Crashaw the conjunction is fortunate and decisive. The "genius for excess" that has been cited as characteristic of the Spanish temperament is also a definitive quality of the Baroque poems of Crashaw.[18] We have seen it manifested in poems as diverse as "Musicks Duell" and "The Weeper" and with varying success; at times, no doubt, the excess is more in evidence than the genius. In the poems that reflect the further impact of the mystical tradition of the *via affirmativa*— notably the three major poems here and the Ode on a Prayer Book—we see emotional fervor join with religious ecstasy to produce an art of Baroque plenitude. For Crashaw the poems represent an artistically ultimate, if not chronologically final, achievement. Just as his life demonstrates the progression of a pilgrim moving from his religious home in Canterbury through a "stateless" existence, finally to be settled near Rome, so his poetry is expressive of an analogous transition. Yet, Crashaw does not so much depart from his artistic roots as he transcends them, realizing in the Teresa poems an art that illustrates his poetic heritage and his own particular genius.

The three poems on Teresa (and a fourth of less distinct focus titled "A Song") form a notable group in the 1652 *Carmen Deo Nostro* and are very nearly at the textual center of that collection. The first two, "A Hymn to the Name and Honor of the Admirable Sainte Teresa" and "An Apologie for the fore-going Hymne," were first published in 1646. In 1648, and again in 1652, they were joined by "The Flaming Heart Upon the Book and Picture of the seraphicall saint, Teresa" and the "Song."[19] The Hymn is undoubtedly the first composed of the Teresa poems, and it may have been written as early as 1638.[20] If so, these poems, though limited in number, provide strong poetic evidence of the continuing impact of St. Teresa on Crashaw over the final decade of his life.

The Hymn is the longest and most satisfying of the three major Teresa poems, and it is one of the most successful poems in the whole of Crashaw's canon.[21] It is the most encompassing in its treatment of the life and mystical death of St. Teresa and is the origin of some crucial motifs developed in the remaining tributes to Teresa. One of these motifs is an overtly sexual one, for in these poems, particularly in the Hymn and "The Flaming Heart," the experience of mystical ecstasy is linguistically linked to a sensuous experience, and the roles of Teresa in the three poems reflect a varying and developing sexual identity.[22] None of this should be surprising given the mystical and Baroque traditions already explored in this study, for the conjunction of sensuality and religious ecstasy seems almost inevitable. Simone Weil defends the mystic's use of the language of love as fitting and proper, and argues that mystical love is intimately tied to the Incarnation. Her words are thus particularly apt for Crashaw: "The longing to love the beauty of the world in a human being is essentially the longing for the Incarnation. It is mistaken if it thinks it is anything else. The Incarnation alone can satisfy it. It is therefore wrong to reproach the mystics, as has been done sometimes, because they use love's language. It is theirs by right. Others only borrow it."[23] Crashaw's own adoption of love's language is particularly conscious and purposeful, confirming his desire to evoke an earthly experience in order better to approximate a mystical one.

The full title of the Hymn as printed in 1652 identifies the complex sexuality of the role of St. Teresa and hints as well at the development of this role in the three poems: "A Hymn to the Name and Honor of the Admirable Sainte Teresa, Foundresse of the Reformation of the Discalced Carmelites, both men and Women; A Woman for Angelicall heigth of speculation, for Masculine courage of performance, more than a woman. Who Yet a child, out ran maturity, and durst plott a Martyrdome." St. Teresa is said to be a woman, yet more than a woman, and the transcendent characteristic is tied both to her "Angelicall heigth of speculation" and to her "Masculine courage of performance." There is thus at least a hint in the title itself of three distinct sexual roles: the feminine, the neuter, and the masculine. Crashaw's aim to join mysticism and sensuality is one of the principal achievements of the Teresa poems, and his careful working out of the ecstatic and sexual roles of St. Teresa adds subtlety and complexity to his effort.[24]

The Hymn is divided into three main concerns: Teresa's early life and the singular importance of her desire for martyrdom among the Moors (lines 1–64); her experience of a "milder MARTYRDOM" through a mystical death and union with God (65–109); and her final death and entry into heaven to be among the blessed (109–82).[25]

The first part of the Hymn is drawn largely from the first chapter of Teresa's *Vida*, where she describes her early life and her early fascination with martyrdom. The opening lines, however, are fully Crashaw's own and have been justly praised for their authority and control: "Love, thou art Absolute sole lord/OF LIFE and DEATH." To prove the superiority of love the poet goes to an unexpected source. Traditionally the lordship of love was demonstrated most persuasively in the martyrs who made the ultimate sacrifice of themselves for love. The poem describes these traditional martyrs in strong and masculine terms:

> old Souldiers, Great and tall,
> Ripe Men of Martyrdom, that could reach down
> With strong armes, their triumphant crown,
> Such as could with lusty breath
> Speak lowd into the face of death
> Their Great LORD'S glorious name. (4-9)

These are martyrs further characterized by "spatious Bosomes" and by "blood and sweat." In this instance, however, love proves its priority by finding a different and more intimate residence, "a private seat,/Making his mansion in the mild/And milky soul of a soft child" (12-14). Age is one crucial difference in the roles identified thus far, the "old Souldiers" contrasting markedly with the "milky soul of a soft child." The implicit sexual identities are notable as well: the soldiers are strong, lusty, loud, masculine; the child is soft, mild, passive, feminine.

In the portrait of Teresa here, a kind of divinely intuited perception of what she must do precedes rational understanding. Almost before she has learned to say "Martyr" she wishes to be one; before she understands why such an experience needs to be undertaken or what it means, she is urged toward her action: "Nor has she e're yet understood/Why to show love, she should shed blood/Yet though she cannot tell you why,/She can LOVE, and she can DY" (21-24). Much in the first section of the poem substantiates the triumphant claim of the opening lines, that Love is "Absolute sole lord/OF LIFE and DEATH." Later, the evidence of love's status will be felt through the joyous ecstasy of divine union. Here, however, the action of the child Teresa confirms the strength and dominance of love:

> Yet has she'a HEART dares hope to prove
> How much lesse strong is DEATH then LOVE.
>   Be love but there; let poor six yeares
> Be pos'd with the maturest Feares
> Man trembles at, you straight shall find
> LOVE knowes no nonage, nor the MIND.
> 'Tis LOVE, not YEARES or LIMBS that can
> Make the Martyr, or the man. (27–34)

There is passion and emotional heat in the opening section, but it falls far short of the ecstatic peaks of the second part of the poem, and the more subdued sensuous impact is appropriate to the youth of the girl Teresa and the nature of her early experience. Her heart, nonetheless, burns with "brave heates" and her "weake brest heaves with strong desire." So intense is her passion for love and death that "she breathes All fire."

The fire of her longing tempts her away from home, for in the poem, as in the *Vida*, martyrdom invites her toward life (and possibly death) among the Moors. There she will trade her life for an "unvalued Diadem," there she will "teach them how to live/In him: or, if they this deny/For him she'l teach them how to DY" (52–54). The closing lines of the first part are more emotional and are written as if with the excitement and determination of the child:

> FAREWEL then, all the world! Adieu.
> TERESA is no more for you.
> Farewell, all pleasures, sports, and joyes,
> (Never till now esteemed toyes)
> Farewell what ever deare may bee,
> MOTHER'S armes or FATHER'S knee
> Farewell house, and farewell home!
> SHE'S for the Moores, and MARTYRDOM. (57–64)

The images effectively juxtapose the simplicity and ordinariness of what Teresa will leave with the audacity and magnitude of what she seeks. Leaving home and pleasures and sports and joys, she seeks martyrdom, and to replace the comfort and gentleness of loving arms or the security of a father's knee, she will find the much more violent embrace of the Moors. Although Teresa feels obviously guided in her mission, she acts within the bounds of human considerations. As Robert Petersson observes, she thus far "moves about in the Order of Nature, only later to become a part of the Order of Grace."[26]

We are led firmly to the conclusion of line 64 largely because we understand the determination, energy, and passion of this "soft child." The martyrdom she finds is not, however, of the traditional sort, and it is not the overtly physical kind described in the opening lines. Beginning in line 65 the poet steps in to redirect Teresa's efforts toward a different, "milder" martyrdom, and, as the poem confirms, it is Christ the Spouse whose call she will follow:

> SWEET, not so fast! lo thy fair Spouse
> Whom thou seekst with so swift vowes,
> Calls thee back, and bidds thee come
> T'embrace a milder MARTYRDOM. (65–68)

Teresa is not to experience a death from enemies who would strike her with brutal, physical force; she is, rather, to be "love's victime; and must dy/A death more mysticall and high" (75–76). Christ is both spouse and sacred Cupid, for "His is the DART must make the DEATH/Whose stroke shall tast thy hallow'd breath" (79–80). It is not Christ, however, who unleashes the dart of love; following Teresa's own account, the "Fitt executioners" are "The fair'st and first-born sons of fire/Blest SERAPHIM, [who] shall leave their quire/And turn love's souldiers, upon THEE/To exercise their archerie" (93–96).

A premature earthly death is denied; in its place is a more lasting "death more mysticall and high." Love would have been revealed through the first kind of death, but now it plays a more complex role. It is love that causes the mystical death that must be experienced in order for love to be evident. Love is at once the motivation and the goal. The mystical union of the soul with God produces emotional heights that far exceed the heat and thirst and fire of the first section.[27] Indeed, the ecstasy can be described only in terms that give full reign to the analogous sensuous experience. In the *Vida* Teresa explicitly confirms the intermingling of corporeal and spiritual joy and pain, and in her own comments on it she does not avoid the language of love and the senses: "it is such a deare, delightfull kind of entercourse, which passes heer between the Soule, and Almightie God, as I beseech him of his infinit goodnes, that he will give some touch, or tast of it, to whosoever shall beleive, that I lye."[28] Crashaw implicitly confirms the same inevitable analogy through his poetic language, as the moment of religious ecstasy is, as well, the emotional and sensuous apex of the poem:

> O how oft shalt thou complain
> Of a sweet and subtle PAIN.
> Of intolerable JOYES;
> Of a DEATH, in which who dyes
> Loves his death, and dyes again.
> And would for ever so be slain.
> And lives, and dyes; and knowes not why
> To live, But that he thus may never leave to DY.
>   How kindly will thy gentle HEART
> Kisse the sweetly-killing DART!
> And close in his embraces keep
> Those delicious Wounds, that weep
> Balsom to heal themselves with. (97–109)

Teresa is here the passive recipient of the love of her Spouse Christ. The wound of love she experiences is the climactic and oxymoronic figure that completes the paradox of love/death so dominant in the poem from its beginning.[29] It is, furthermore, the fitting poetic climax to the mission of the six-year-old child. Denied the single death of the martyr, she finds frequent "deaths" in the mystical union of her soul with God.

The final section of the poem introduces us to still a third kind of death, one that joins features of the martyr's physical death and the mystic's ecstatic death. This death, like that of the martyr, is a literal one, involving the separation of soul and body. Unlike the martyr's death, however, it is gentle and pleasant and thus seizes on the emotional and spiritual pleasures of mystical death. The death of Teresa's corporeal nature is imaged as the melting of "thy Soul's sweet mansion,"

> Like a soft lump of incense, hasted
> By too hott a fire, and wasted
> Into perfuming clouds, so fast
> Shalt thou exhale to Heavn at last
> In a resolving SIGH. (113–17)

The last sixty lines of the poem imaginatively portray her entry into

heaven and the community of the blessed who greet her there: the
Virgin, Christ, Angels, and on a different level, her own works and
suffering.

Praz has commented about the final section that there is
"something detached and of a descriptive nature in this composition: the poet does not yet possess the adequate lyric heat for the
mystical experience."[30] No doubt the final section lacks the "lyric
heat" Praz refers to, and it does not entirely avoid the sense of
anticlimax coming after the tightly integrated and developing
emotional intensity of the poem through line 109. But the "mystical
experience" of the poem is more nearly approximated in the
second part of the Hymn, and that part is, appropriately, the most
notable for its emotional energy. The final lines are more imaginative than visionary, less a beatific vision than a joyful anticipation
of union and reunion in heaven after death.

Teresa maintains her role as Christ's beloved, an image quite
conventional in view of her life as a nun yet particularly consistent
with her prominent sexual identity in the poem. Christ is her King
and Spouse, and the active working of His love in her, as well as the
resulting influence that it has on other religious devotees, is imaged
in terms that, though gentle, are unequivocally sexual:

> Sons of thy vowes,
> The virgin-births with which thy soveraign spouse
> Made fruitfull thy fair soul, goe now
> And with them all about thee bow
> To Him, put on (hee'l say) put on
> (My rosy love) That thy rich zone
> Sparkling with the sacred flames
> Of thousand soules, whose happy names
> Heav'n keeps upon thy score. (167–75)

Christ's address to his beloved recalls, in its language, rhythm, and
repetition, the erotic context of the Song of Songs, and the ending
of the poem thus adds to the extraordinary juxtaposition of the
sacred and the sensual prominent throughout the Hymn.

In "The Flaming Heart" Crashaw is especially attentive to the
works of St. Teresa and to his own role as one who responds to her
influence. He does not neglect his participation in the ultimate
section of the Hymn, but it is played down, for the poet is not
alone, as he is at the end of "The Flaming Heart," but is part of a
company still influenced by the saint. Teresa's works, in which is

"writt/Love's noble history," serve both to clothe her soul in heaven and to "feed our soules" on earth:

> Each heavnly word by whose hid flame
> Our hard Hearts shall strike fire, the same
> Shall flourish on thy browes. and be
> Both fire to us and flame to thee;
> Whose light shall live bright in thy FACE
> By glory, in our hearts by grace. (159-64)

The final lines reinforce the continuing pattern and influence set by Teresa, both in life and in death, and draw concise attention to the inevitable Christian paradoxes of living and dying. Portraying for a final time the pleasures of Teresa's heaven, Crashaw urges that those "who in *death* would *live* to see,/Must learn in *life* to *dy* like thee" (italics mine).

Perhaps the most significant achievement of the Hymn is its effective control of several themes and motifs, and within a context that gives expression to religious and poetic exuberance. Crashaw never loses his grip in this poem, although he might easily have done so.[31] On the contrary, the poem works through clearly distinguished divisions and integrates successfully the sensual and religious contexts fundamental to its meaning. In the reader's poetic experience, as in the personal experience of St. Teresa, emotional and sensuous excitement leads to a fuller perception of the divine.

The "Apologie for the fore-going Hymne" is a defense of two features of the Hymn: the fact that the poem is written in the "weak and worthlesse song" of his English instead of "other tongues . . . tun'd so high" and, conversely, the fact that it contains implicit pro-Spanish sentiments even though written by an Englishman. Crashaw's principal answer to the first objection is ultimately linked to his answer to the second; it is not language or nationality that is important but love: "love is eloquence." Consequently, much of the poem advances the transcendent quality of Teresa's work and influence, beyond time, and language, and geographical boundaries.

In the "Apologie" Teresa's own role is much less prominent, and thus one motif developed in the Hymn—her sexual identity—is in this poem much less apparent. The poet's primary aim is to deny the importance of traditional distinctions, and the emphasis throughout is therefore on the sense of unity—or, in sexual terms, a neutrality—resulting from a common faith in Christ. St. Paul's admonition that "there is neither Jew nor Greek, there is neither bond nor free, there is neither male nor female: for ye are all one in Christ Jesus" (Gal. 3:28) finds a particular parallel in Crashaw's denial of present distinctions: "Souls are not SPANIARDS too, one freindly floud/Of BAPTISM blends them all into a blood./ CHRIST'S faith makes but one body of all soules/And love's that body's soul" (15–18).

The implications of neuter sexuality are enhanced a few moments later, as the poet describes the inebriating effect resulting from the "wine of love" delivered by the Spanish saint. Although some drink turns men into beasts, subhuman forms, this drink turns men into angels, suprahuman forms. The reference in the full title of the Hymn to Teresa's "Angelicall heigth of speculation" making her "more then a woman" has an analogue here: "Some drink," we are told, turns "men to beasts, o then/Drink we till we prove more, not lesse, then men,/And turn not beasts, but Angels" (35–37).

The "Apologie" consists of two parts, both involving the poet quite immediately but with differing degrees of emotional intensity. The first section (1–28) is the defense ("apology") proper, calling on love to minimize differences and thereby eliminate prejudices: "let no fond Hate/Of names and wordes, so farr præjudicate" (13–14). Teresa's works are to be highly regarded, not because they are from Spain but because they transcend their Spanish origin: "O 'tis not spanish, but 'tis heav'n she speaks!" (23). The heaven of her language works its effect on the "wondring reader's brest" and produces the beginning of a divine flight away from the limitations of earth.

What was in the Hymn imaged in terms of a religious/sexual ecstasy is in the "Apologie" viewed as divine inebriation. The second half of the poem thus grows in its excitement as the poem grows thematically with the motif of the "wine of love." The poet seeks a special kind of wine, a blood-wine, that transcends the wine of grapes, just as his divine inebriation far excels the drunken, and debilitating, state of ordinary men:

> Let the king
> Me ever into these his cellars bring
> Where flowes such wine as we can have of none
> But HIM who trod the wine-presse all alone:
> Wine of youth, life, and the sweet Deaths of love;

> Wine of immortall mixture; which can prove
> It's Tincture from the rosy nectar; wine
> That can exalt weak EARTH; and so refine
> Our dust, that at one draught, mortality
> May drink it self up, and forget to dy. (37–46)

In this final section of the poem there is a remarkable meeting of sources and influences, each fully integrated with the others and with Crashaw's own perspective to form a statement that transcends the earthly limits above which the poet seeks to rise. The source of the initial lines is the Song of Songs 2:4, and probably the version in the Vulgate: "Introduxit me in cellam vinariam, ordinavit in me charitatem" (He brought me into the wine cellar, he appointed in me love). It is also likely, as others have noted, that Crashaw knew the commentaries of Teresa on the passage, particularly those found in her *Interior Castle* and *Conceptions of the Love of God*.[32] In *Conceptions* she interprets the biblical passage in a long commentary that Crashaw may have recalled in his poem. Near the end of her remarks she focuses on the inebriated joys the Bride will experience from the King:

His will is that she shall drink, and become inebriated with all the wines that are in the storehouse of God. Let her rejoice in those joys; let her marvel at His wonders; let her not fear to lose her life through drinking beyond the capacity of her weak nature; let her die in this paradise of delights. Blessed is the death that brings with it such a life! And this is indeed what it does; for so great are the marvelous things learned by the soul, without its knowing how, that it is beside itself, as the soul itself says in the words: "He set in order charity in me."[33]

The imagery of line 40 is drawn from Isaiah 63:3 ("I have troden the winepresse alone, and of the people there was none with me") and is given additional force through the typological association of Christ with the "I" and the winepress as the winepress of the cross, from which flows the wine-blood of redemption.[34]

A final likely influence on the language and perspective of the poem is St. François de Sales. Of particular note are St. François's comments on two kinds of inebriation, the earthly one turning men into beasts, the divine one turning them into angels:

To be inebriated is to contemplate so frequently and so ardently as to be quite out of self to be wholly in God. O holy and sacred inebriation, which, contrarily to corporal inebriation, does not alienate us from the spiritual sense, but from the corporal senses; does not dull or besot us, but *angelicizes* and in a sort deifies us; putting us out of ourselves, not to abase us and rank us with beasts, as terrestrial drunkenness does, but to raise us above ourselves and range us with angels, so that we may live more in God then in ourselves, being attentive to and occupied in seeing his beauty and being united to his goodness by love![35]

The final section of the "Apologie" is all the more remarkable in its conciseness because it effectively welds biblical texts and contexts with various but related commentary. The wine of love produces a dazzling and unearthly effect comparable to that resulting from the wound of love in the Hymn. The whole is a rich portrait of the wine that can lead to divine ecstasy. Like the wound, this wine brings "sweet Deaths of love" and through those deaths it brings another life: "mortality/May drink it self up, and forget to dy."

"The Flaming Heart" is the third of the Teresa poems, and in several ways it is the fitting climax, not only to this group of three but also to the poetic and personal development revealed in the whole of Crashaw's canon. Beginning slowly, even mechanically, it builds to a great crescendo, forming in its final lines what has been called one of Crashaw's "few perfectly realized . . . passages."[36] Unlike the Hymn, where the poet's role is modest and impersonal, or the "Apologie," where it is subdued by the imagery of wine and love, life and death, "The Flaming Heart" concludes with the full and unrestrained participation of the speaker. Before, it was Teresa or an impersonal "we" who sought the revelation of divine ecstasy; in the final poem the poet is openly and passionately involved. He pleads for the mystical experience for himself and approaches divine understanding through the passionate exuberance of the close of the poem. Mario Praz comments that "in the whole course of seventeenth-century literature there is no higher expression of that spiritualization of sense which is condensed here in a portentous, dizzy soaring of red-hot images."[37]

It is difficult to argue with confidence that the Hymn to Teresa looks forward to the next two poems; the uncertainty of dating makes such a claim particularly problematic. Nonetheless, "The Flaming Heart" can be approached from the vantage point of the Hymn, for it works with and effectively varies similar motifs, images, and themes. At the heart of the two major Teresa poems is

Teresa's experience of the transverberation. In the Hymn we are led from her experience of mystical death to an imaginative portrait of her final death and heavenly life. In "The Flaming Heart" mystical death for her leads to a desire for mystical death by the poet. The action of love causes in both poems "delicious Wounds" and a flaming heart, leading to the ecstasy of joy and pain described so vividly in the Hymn.

Of greater complexity, because it involves such a profound change, is the implicit sexual identity Teresa assumes in the two poems. The impact cannot be avoided, since both poems (as well as the "Apologie") adopt so thoroughly the language of love to give insight to the experience of ecstasy. In the Hymn Teresa is portrayed in a passive and conventionally feminine role; she is, both on earth and in heaven, the recipient of love from her Spouse Christ, living and dying in a way that separates her from more traditionally masculine action. In the "Apologie" the concern with Teresa and her sexual identity is muted, but in the third poem it receives its most complex and climactic treatment.

The extended title of the third Teresa poem suggests that "The Flaming Heart" was written about a painting of the saint: "The Flaming Heart Upon the Book and Picture of the seraphicall saint Teresa, (As She is Usually Expressed with a Seraphim biside her.)." The most famous portrait of St. Teresa's ecstasy is Bernini's sculpture, but Crashaw would not have seen it. It is quite possible, in fact, that he is concentrating less on a single portrait than on how she is "usually expressed" in art.[38] We do not require outside pictorial aid to discover what the usual portraits revealed, for the poem makes the essential features abundantly clear. Typically, Teresa was seen as the weakened and passive recipient of the dart of love thrust by the seraphim, a view that Crashaw poetically reiterates in his Hymn. And it is precisely this identity that Crashaw, in his third poem, challenges. After identifying saint and seraphim the poet urges that their roles ought to be reversed:

> Readers, be rul'd by me; and make
> Here a well-plac't and wise mistake,
> You must transpose the picture quite,
> And spell it wrong to read it right;
> Read HIM for her, and her for him;
> And call the SAINT the SERAPHIM. (7–12)

Addressing the painter directly, the poet suggests more exactly where the mistakes occur. In essence, they result from an attempt to make Teresa too passive, too feminine. The painter, Crashaw says, has unkindly erred in showing "This faint shade for HER" (22). The portrait "mockes with female FROST love's manly flame"; by looking at the painting "One would suspect thou meant'st to paint/Some weak, inferiour, woman saint" (24-26). All of this, the poet suggests, is wrong; Teresa should have the features of the masculine seraphim, and she should, above all, have his dart.

In the Hymn Teresa receives the dart of love from her spouse Christ, and in that poem sexual and marital imagery is prominent, all of it appropriate for the specifically feminine role she has there. In "The Flaming Heart" Teresa herself is to have the dart and takes on as well the roles of the active lover and the courageous warrior who wounds those who receive her thrust. Confirming her more masculine role, there is a striking conjunction of love and military imagery:

> Give her the DART for it is she
> (Fair youth) shootes both thy shaft and THEE
> Say, all ye wise and well-peirc't hearts
> That live and dy amidst her darts,
> What is't your tastfull spirits doe prove
> In that rare life of Her, and love?
> Say and bear wittnes. Sends she not
> A SERAPHIM at every shott?
> What magazins of immortall ARMES there shine!
> Heavn's great artillery in each love-spun line.
> Give then the dart to her who gives the flame;
> Give him the veil, who kindly takes the shame. (47-58)

In lines that follow, the poet admits that his request may have gone too far. He wills back to the seraphim all of the qualities he previously claimed as more fitting for the saint. It is sufficient, he says, that Teresa retain only the flaming heart: "His be the bravery of all those Bright things,/The glowing cheekes, the glistering wings;/The Rosy hand, the radiant DART;/Leave HER alone THE FLAMING HEART" (65-68). Crashaw does not, however, dismiss his concern with Teresa's more masculine role. Indeed, as if to underscore that role, he takes what has been a feminine virtue and turns it into a masculine one. With an emphasis that effectively joins the Hymn and this poem, he argues that Teresa's "flaming heart," which was before the most obvious sign of her reception of

Christ's love, can now be turned into a strong and active force.
Leave her the flaming heart, the poet says,

> and thou shalt leave her
> Not one loose shaft but love's whole quiver.
> For in love's feild was never found
> A nobler weapon than a WOUND.
> Love's passives are his activ'st part.
> The wounded is the wounding heart. (69–74)

This complex response to the passivity/activity of the saint is
repeated a few lines later, as the poet moves closer to that portion
of the poem where he desires the saint's flaming influence to touch
his own heart: "Live here, great HEART; and love and dy and
kill;/And bleed and wound; and yeild and conquer still" (79–80).

The consummate portrait of Teresa's sexual identity is seen in
the lines that close the poem (85–108), as Crashaw allows the
reader only to overhear his words and addresses the saint directly.
Since he pleads for the action of Teresa on him, her role retains its
forceful character: her "art" will be wielded "Upon this carcasse of
a hard, cold, hart"; her "scatter'd shafts of light" will be directed
against his breast and "take away from me my self and sin." But in
fact the language of love is muted, and we are less aware of the
analogy than we are of the mystical experience itself. Seeking the
mystical vision, Crashaw drops all masks. Metaphoric language is
unavoidable, of course, but it has a directness, immediacy, and
variety unseen elsewhere in Crashaw's poetry:

> O thou undanted daughter of desires!
> By all thy dowr of LIGHTS and FIRES;
> By all the eagle in thee, all the dove;
> By all thy lives and deaths of love;
> By thy larg draughts of intellectuall day,
> And by thy thirsts of love more large then they;
> By all thy brim-fill'd Bowles of feirce desire
> By thy last Morning's draught of liquid fire;
> By the full kingdome of that finall kisse
> That seiz'd thy parting Soul, and seal'd thee his;
> By all the heav'ns thou hast in him
> (Fair sister of the SERAPHIM!)
> By all of HIM we have in THEE;
> Leave nothing of my SELF in me.
> Let me so read thy life, that I
> Unto all life of mine may dy. (93–108)

Against the passion and personal involvement of these lines, we can instructively set the lines of "A Song." Like the Teresa poems that precede it, "A Song" describes the mystical death that leads to life. But its language and rhythm are flat and mechanical; the experience is described but not felt. The second part, for example, never probes beneath a superficial wit:

> Though still I dy, I live again;
> Still longing so to be still slain,
> So gainfull is such losse of breath,
> I dy even in desire of death.
>   Still live in me this loving strife
> Of living DEATH and dying LIFE.
> For while thou sweetly slayest me
> Dead to my selfe, I live in Thee.

The closing lines of "The Flaming Heart" confirm that Teresa's role is at once passive and active, and demonstrate the theological basis for the sexual images advanced in the poems. She is the feminine recipient of divine love in the Hymn and the active begetter of love in "The Flaming Heart," for Christ (Love) first acts *on* her and then continues to act *through* her (and her works) on others. The active role of the saint is borne out in the receptive role of the poet. It is, as well, a final example of a complex reciprocity we have seen in other forms in Crashaw's work. Christ acts on Teresa who, in turn, directs her response upward toward Him and downward toward others. The poet responds to her example by praising both her and Christ and thus confirms the value of her life and death and the efficacy of her action and Christ's. Through the poet's mystical death, Teresa and Christ would experience a form of life.

Epilogue

THE life and poetry of Richard Crashaw reveal, as I have attempted to show, a pattern of analogous progression, one which begins to take him increasingly away from his English and Anglican background. The young Crashaw was evidently a good student, establishing his scholastic capabilities at Charterhouse and extending them through two degrees at Cambridge. The schoolboy read his lessons and his poets well, for it is clear that early on his poetry was regarded with some acclaim. When he gently chides himself for being slow to produce his "two greene Apricockes" in contrast to his friend Cowley's "Hesperides," the response is appropriate for the occasion and the comparison, but in fact Crashaw's epigrams, as well as other pieces, prove both his youthful interest in poetry and the considerable recognition that some of the early work attained. That poetry is, with few exceptions, in the best traditions available to and followed by other poets of his day. Crashaw was younger than twenty when he wrote the poems on the gunpowder treason and the king's coronation, the paraphrases of the Psalms, the admirable elegy on Ashton, and a certain though unknown number of the English and Latin epigrams. His admission to Pembroke College and his almost immediate invitation to begin contributing to university volumes were likely influenced by some knowledge of his poetic accomplishments. Crashaw's selection as the poet to write the tribute to Lancelot Andrewes in the publication of the renowned Anglican preacher's *XCVI Sermons* in 1632, at a time when he was not yet, or was only barely, twenty, is even more convincing evidence of the public recognition of his work. Furthermore, he was honored by the publication of *Epigrammatum Sacrorum Liber*, in 1634, when he was still only twenty-one or twenty-two. There is thus more than enough evidence to justify Lloyd's favorable portrait of Crashaw's "Divine fancy," grounded in Charterhouse and "famous" at Pembroke and Peterhouse.

The fame of Crashaw within the university community was undoubtedly enhanced through his frequent appearances in the various memorial and congratulatory volumes produced by the university for the "occasions" of the day. During Crashaw's Pembroke years, especially, the poet seems to have been writing mostly under different kinds of obligation, either the weekly epigrams drawn from prayer book readings or the elegiac or celebrative pieces prompted by contemporary events. Such frequent poetic exercises encouraged the poet's interest in form and style and proved his versatility within relatively restricting genres. Other features of university life had further effects on the development of Crashaw as man and poet. At Cambridge Crashaw had extended and intimate contact with persons of a similar temperament and religious inclination, both within the university proper and at Little Gidding, and the university years thus provided abundant nourishment for Laudian sensibilities. The university was also an encouraging environment for one whose poetic and spiritual models were drawn not only from within England but from beyond its borders as well. Marino and St. Teresa were comfortably absorbed by the multilingual student and poet and could be read and appreciated along with Spenser or Donne or Herbert. The poetry from the Cambridge years, as we have seen, comes increasingly to reflect the richly varied traditions to which Crashaw was attentive. The occasional poems do not deserve neglect, but by the mid-1630s Crashaw had moved on to other and more ambitious poetic subjects. The poems written over the last decade and a half of his life are his most important and are the most revealing of his spiritual and poetic development. The stateliness of the Renaissance tradition and the intellectual core of the Metaphysical tradition are increasingly muted by the louder and more emotional rhetoric of the Baroque. The capacity for emotional and sensuous luxury, encouraged by the Laudian environments of Charterhouse and Cambridge, crescendoes under the influence of the rhetoric of ecstasy in St. Teresa. The hymns and the Teresa poems, which surely represent the final stage of Crashaw's spiritual and literary development, contain, with few exceptions, those qualities of the Baroque Crashaw that have become best known—sensuous analogies, an emotional, sometimes ecstatic tone, abundance and repetition. In view of the varied but steady development of Crashaw's poetry, a development that seems to me, in its essential features, unarguable, the final lines of "The Flaming Heart" are particularly interesting and instructive.

Those lines—with their extraordinary excitement, their passionate and intimate rhetoric, their plea for the dissolution of self in a mystical union modeled after the experience of the Spanish Catholic saint—would appear to put Crashaw at his farthest remove from his English and Anglican heritage. If we think, for immediate contrast, of the earliest epigrams or some of the simple and straightforward secular pieces, we realize how far Crashaw has advanced toward the increasingly Baroque temper of his work. We would suppose, therefore, that his most characteristically Baroque and ecstatic passage, probably written on the Continent during the last two years of his life, is the most distant from his literary and religious roots. But Crashaw, to the end, is capable of assimilating otherwise disparate traditions. The closing lines of "The Flaming Heart," as Austin Warren demonstrated many years ago, reflect both the rhythm and language of that most English of texts, *The Book of Common Prayer.*[1] A portion of the Litany must have been somewhere in Crashaw's mind as he created his fiery lines:

> By the mystery of thy holy incarnation, by the holy
> nativity and circumcision, by thy baptism, fasting, and temptation.
>> Good Lord deliver us.
> By thine agony and bloody sweat, by thy cross and passion,
> by thy precious death and burial, by thy glorious
> resurrection and ascension, and by the coming of the Holy Ghost.
>> Good Lord deliver us.

In the earlier discussion of the artistic setting for Crashaw's verse I suggested that his singular achievement among English poets is not to be found simply in the Baroque quality of his work but in the often unique fusion of diverse influences and traditions that his poetry reveals. This diversity is apparent both among poems of a similar genre or theme (the elegies, for example) and within single poems (the "Apologie" on St. Teresa or the Ode on a Prayer Book, among others). In a number of ways the most compelling example of Crashaw's integrative poetic is seen here. Crashaw's recollection (whether conscious or unconscious) of lines from a book so intimately tied to the life and literature of a country he had left suggests for a final time the richly varied and complex quality of his art and his ability to create a unified vision from varied elements. The rhetoric of the Litany is essentially public and ritualistic, achieving its effect through repetition and communal recitation. The passage cited here moves progressively through events in the life of Jesus, but there is little marked advance in emotion or excitement. The "Good Lord" addressed in the Litany is the Savior to whom ritual prayers are to be offered on a continuing basis; the specific lines of prayer ("Good Lord deliver us") function to modulate the rhythm and emotion of the Litany, effectively controlling the tone and reinforcing the public quality of the prayer. Crashaw's poem contains no such modulation. The stately eloquence of Anglican ritual is, in Crashaw's radical transformation, charged with the energy of personal involvement and pleading. "Us" in the Litany becomes "me" in the poem, historical events are supplanted by vivid and sensuous metaphors, chronological order is replaced by an emotional one, as the poet approaches ever closer to the ecstatic heights he seeks. The lines addressed to St. Teresa, the "undanted daughter of desires," build steadily to the final climax, the urging of a quite singular and ecstatic experience.

In this most Baroque passage Crashaw is, in a sense, also quite English in his indebtedness to the prayer book, and it is this capacity both to adopt and to transform diverse influences and materials that contributes to the unique quality of Crashaw's art. Crashaw the man and poet made the crucial pilgrimages I have described in this study—from Canterbury to Rome, from pithy or simple poetic passages to extended and exuberant ones. But his poetry taken as a whole is vivid testimony to his ability to draw on and integrate different traditions and to enhance them through his own distinct voice.

Notes and References

Chapter One

1. Arthur Joseph Slavin, *The Precarious Balance: English Government and Society*, The Borzoi History of England, Vol. 3, 1450–1640 (New York: Knopf, 1973), p. 304.
2. Slavin, pp. 316–23.
3. *DNB*, "William Laud."
4. *DNB*, "John Cosin."
5. *DNB*, "William Crashaw."
6. From the copy of William Crashaw's will in the Public Records Office (Hele 97). See also L. C. Martin, ed. *The Poems English, Latin, and Greek of Richard Crashaw*, 2nd ed. (Oxford: The Clarendon Press, 1957), pp. xviii–xix.
7. The first remark is contained in *A Sermon Preached at the Crosse* (1608), the second in William Crashaw's will. I have quoted from a copy of the sermon in the Bancroft Library of the University of California, Berkeley.
8. Cf. Austin Warren, *Richard Crashaw: A Study in Baroque Sensibility* (University, La: Louisiana State Univ. Press, 1939), pp. 210–15, for a review of William Crashaw's writing career.
9. Martin, p. xvi.
10. Warren, *Richard Crashaw*, p. 210.
11. E. I. Watkin suggests that William Crashaw is not necessarily Puritan in a perceptive article, "William Crashaw's Influence on His Son," *Dublin Review* 223(1953): 1–25. We also know that Crashaw was attacked by a Puritan spokesman on at least one occasion. Henry Ainsworth, a "fine type of Elizabethan puritan" (*DNB*), published a 1608 work titled *Counterpoyson*, containing refutations of various Anglican preachers, including Crashaw.
12. From the copy in the Bodleian Library, Oxford (Malone 297). Also cited in Martin, p. xviii. Martin's "Introduction" and Warren's study are the two best modern sources of details of Crashaw's life. I am indebted to each.
13. Cited in Martin, p. 415.

14. Gerald S. Davies, *Charterhouse in London* (London: J. Murray, 1921), p. 256.

15. Cited in Martin, p. 415.

16. In George Walton Williams, ed., *The Complete Poetry of Richard Crashaw* (1970; rpt. New York: Norton, 1974), p. 639.

17. Davies, pp. 232–33.

18. See Martin, p. xcii.

19. Davies, p. 251.

20. Warren, *Richard Crashaw*, pp. 22–23.

21. Ibid., p. 215.

22. Cited in Martin, p. 417.

23. Cf. Warren, *Richard Crashaw*, pp. 23–24.

24. Williams, *The Complete Poetry*, pp. 624–29.

25. Charles Henry Cooper, *Annals of Cambridge* (Cambridge, Eng.: Warwick and Co., 1845), III, 263–64.

26. Martin, p. 438.

27. Austin Warren, "Crashaw and Peterhouse," *TLS*, 13 August 1931, p. 621.

28. Austin Warren, "Richard Crashaw: 'Catechist and Curate,'" *Modern Philology* 32(1935): 264, 267.

29. Williams, *The Complete Poetry*, p. 651.

30. Martin, p. 416.

31. Peter Peckard, *A Life of Nicholas Ferrar* (London: Joseph Masters, 1852), p. 94. The *Life* is an abridgment of Peckard's *Memoirs of the Life of Mr. Nicholas Ferrar* (Cambridge, Eng., 1790).

32. Peckard, pp. 108–109.

33. Ibid., p. 129.

34. *DNB*, "Nicholas Ferrar."

35. Peckard, p. 143.

36. Martin asserts that the letter, currently housed in the Cambridge Library as MS. 7316, is "the only piece of English prose from Crashaw's hand known to exist" (p. xxv). That is, however, a point of debate. W. W. Greg stated in 1932 that there is "no reason to doubt that the letter is Crashaw's, but it is not autograph" (*English Literary Autographs 1550–1650* [Oxford, Eng., 1932; rpt. Nendeln, Liechtenstein: Kraus, 1968], No. XCIX). More recently, Mr. Hilton Kelliher of the Department of Manuscripts of the British Library indicated to me in conversations during May 1979 that he believes the letter is not autograph.

37. Cited in Thomas A. Walker, *Peterhouse* (Cambridge, Eng.: W. Heffer & Sons, 1935), pp. 55–56.

38. From *Innovations in Religion & Abuses in Government in* [*the*] *University of Cambridge* (British Museum MS. Harley 7019, fol. 73). See also Allan Pritchard, "Puritan Charges against Crashaw and Beaumont," *TLS*, 2 July 1964, p. 578.

39. Cooper, p. 364. Two months prior to this ordinance the university had sent a petition to Parliament asking to be exempted from "Rates and Impositions" and appealing for a recognition of its status as a seat of learning. It called attention to the "sad dejected estate" of the university that was thrown into academic disarray by the growing conflict (see "To the Honourable the Lords and Commons now assembled in the High Court of Parliament. The Humble Petition of the University of Cambridge" [British Museum, *Thomason Tracts*, Vol. 3, fol. 30]). The response of Parliament shows no sympathy for the university's plight.

40. Cooper, p. 364.

41. Walker, p. 58.

42. "Crashaw's Residence at Peterhouse," *TLS*, 3 November 1932, p. 815.

43. See Martin, p. xxxiii.

44. From the MS in the Cambridge Library. See Martin, p. xxxi.

45. Martin, p. xxvii.

46. See Martin's discussion of chronology and dating, pp. lxxxvii–xcii.

47. Kenneth Larsen's article, "Some Light on Richard Crashaw's Final Years in Rome," *Modern Language Review* 66(1971): 492-96, adds important details to our previously sketchy knowledge of Crashaw's final years.

48. Martin, pp. xliv–xlv.

49. Ibid., pp. xci–xcii.

50. Ibid., pp. xxxiv, xlviii.

51. The quoted comments are those of Louis L. Martz, "The Action of the Self: Devotional Poetry in the Seventeenth Century," in Malcolm Bradbury and David Palmer, eds., *Metaphysical Poetry* (Bloomington: Indiana Univ. Press, 1971), p. 117; Frank J. Warnke, *European Metaphysical Poetry* (1961; rpt. New Haven: Yale Univ. Press, 1974), p. 82; T. S. Eliot, "A Note on Richard Crashaw," in *For Lancelot Andrewes* (Garden City, N.Y.: Doubleday, 1929), p. 137.

52. Robert T. Petersson, *The Art of Ecstasy* (1970; rpt. New York: Atheneum, 1974), p. 123.

53. Ruth Wallerstein (*Richard Crashaw: A Study in Style and Poetic Development*, University of Wisconsin Studies in Language and Literature, No. 37 [Madison: Univ. of Wisconsin Press, 1935], pp. 16-55); and George Williamson (*The Donne Tradition* [New York: Farrar, Straus, 1958], p. 113) both see Crashaw moving toward a more profound sense of ecstasy and mysticism in his poetry.

54. *The Wit of Love* (Notre Dame: Univ. of Notre Dame Press, 1969), p. 114.

55. *Four Stages of Renaissance Style* (Garden City, N.Y.: Doubleday, 1955), pp. 57, 33.

56. Warren, *Richard Crashaw*, p. 90.

56a. The more specific source of line 20 is Chaucer's *Canterbury Tales*, General Prologue, line 5: "Whan Zephirus eek with his sweete breeth."

57. Warnke's *European Metaphysical Poetry* and Odette de Mourgues's *Metaphysical Baroque & Précieux Poetry* (Oxford, Eng.: The Clarendon Press, 1953) are cases in point.

58. Warnke, *European Metaphysical Poetry*, pp. 15–16, 82; Earl Miner, *The Metaphysical Mode from Donne to Cowley* (Princeton: Princeton Univ. Press, 1969), p. 186; Joan Bennett, *Five Metaphysical Poets* (Cambridge, Eng.: Cambridge Univ. Press, 1964), pp. vii, 102; Douglas Bush, *English Literature in the Earlier Seventeenth Century, 1600–1660*, 2nd ed. (Oxford, Eng.: The Clarendon Press, 1962), p. 147.

59. James Smith, "On Metaphysical Poetry," in *A Selection from Scrutiny*, ed. F. R. Leavis, Vol. II (Cambridge, Eng.: Cambridge Univ. Press, 1968), p. 162 (originally published in 1933).

60. Smith, p. 161.

61. In his "Life of Cowley," from *Lives of the English Poets* (1779–1781). The comment is reprinted in A. L. Clements, ed., *John Donne's Poetry* (New York: Norton, 1966), p. 107.

62. See "A Seventeenth-Century Theory of Metaphysical Poetry," *Romantic Review* 42(1951): 245–55, and "Metaphysical Poetry and the Poetic of Correspondences," *Journal of the History of Ideas* 14(1953): 221–34; both are reprinted in *Renaissance and Seventeenth-Century Studies* (New York: Columbia Univ. Press, 1964), pp. 29–59.

63. Mazzeo, "Metaphysical Poetry and the Poetic of Correspondences," p. 230.

64. The central place of the witty conceit in estimates of Metaphysical poetry is also suggested by the relationship between the Metaphysical tradition and other, more Continental, aesthetic movements, such as *concettismo* or *seicentismo*. See Joseph Mazzeo, "A Critique of Some Modern Theories of Metaphysical Poetry," *Modern Philology* 50(1952): 88–89.

65. Warnke, *European Metaphysical Poetry*, p. 8.

66. The motto is adapted from the motto of St. François de Sales. See A. F. Allison, "Crashaw and St. François de Sales," *Review of English Studies* 24(1948): 295–302.

67. Cf. Frank Warnke, "Metaphysical Poetry and the European Context," in Bradbury and Palmer, pp. 273–74.

68. Frank Warnke, *Versions of Baroque* (New Haven: Yale Univ. Press, 1972), p. 23.

69. Martz, *The Wit of Love*, pp. 127–28. See also Smith, pp. 168–69, and Warnke, *European Metaphysical Poetry*, p. 6.

70. Warnke, *European Metaphysical Poetry*, p. 3.

71. Miner, p. 188.

72. Sypher, p. 181.

73. R. Lebègue, quoted in de Mourgues, p. 71.

74. Martz, *The Wit of Love*, pp. 116, 135.

75. Cf. Mary Ellen Rickey, *Rhyme and Meaning in Richard Crashaw* (Lexington: Univ. of Kentucky Press, 1961), *passim*.

76. J. P. Hill and E. Caracciolo-Trejo, eds., *Baroque Poetry* (London: J. M. Dent & Sons, 1975), p. xv. See also James V. Mirollo's study, *The Poet of the Marvelous: Giambattista Marino* (New York: Columbia Univ. Press, 1963), pp. 159–60.

77. Warnke, *European Metaphysical Poetry*, p. 23. See also his *Versions of Baroque*, p. 54.

78. *European Metaphysical Poetry*, pp. 82–83.

79. Miner, p. 102.

80. Bush, p. 147.

Chapter Two

1. Martin, p. 415.

2. Cf. Hoyt H. Hudson, *The Epigram in the English Renaissance* (Princeton: Princeton Univ. Press, 1947), pp. 145ff.

3. *Rules and Orders Relating to Charterhouse, And to the Good Government thereof* (London, n.d.), p. 20.

4. The "Introduction" in *The Latin Poetry of English Poets*, ed. J. W. Binns (London: Routledge & Kegan Paul, 1974), pp. viii–ix.

5. Wallerstein, *Richard Crashaw*, p. 9.

6. Warren, *Richard Crashaw*, p. 89.

7. Cf. Leicester Bradner, *Musae Anglicanae* (New York: Modern Language Association, 1940), p. 78.

8. Cf. Warren, *Richard Crashaw*, p. 80.

9. Ibid.

10. Cited in Hoyt Hudson, pp. 10–11.

11. From the copy in the Humanities Research Center, the University of Texas at Austin.

12. George Puttenham, *The Arte of English Poesie* (1589) (Menston, Eng.: The Scolar Press, 1968), p. 43.

13. Cited by Mario Praz, *Studies in Seventeenth-Century Imagery*, 2nd ed. (Rome: Edizioni di Storia e Letteratura, 1964), p. 18.

14. Mario Praz, *The Flaming Heart* (1958; rpt. New York: Norton, 1973), p. 206.

15. "Wit and Mystery: A Revaluation in Medieval Latin Hymnody," *Speculum* 22(1947): 315.

16. Alexander Grosart, ed., *The Complete Works of Richard Crashaw*, The Fuller Worthies Library (London: Printed for Private Circulation, 1873), II, 168.

17. See Warren, "Crashaw's *Epigrammata Sacra*," *JEGP* 33(1934):

233–39; Sister Maris Stella Milhaupt, "The Latin Epigrams of Richard Crashaw," Diss. Univ. of Michigan 1963, pp. 24–36; Kenneth J. Larsen, "Richard Crashaw's *Epigrammata Sacra*," in Binns, pp. 93–98.

18. In his article on the *Epigrammatum* Larsen concludes that a close study of the epigrams reveals increasing attention to the High Anglican emphasis on love and good works as we progress chronologically through the poems.

19. Translations are mine except for those cited as Crashaw's own; I am, however, indebted to the previous work of Milhaupt and Phyllis Bowman in Williams's edition. The numbers of the poems follow Williams's edition.

20. Kathleen Lea, "Conceits," *Modern Language Review* 20(1925): 404.

21. Sir John Denham, *Preface to the Destruction of Troy* (1656), quoted in R. P. Cowl, *The Theory of Poetry in England* (1914; rpt. New York: Phaeton Press, 1970), p. 144.

22. Grosart, II, lxxviii.

23. I do not discuss all of the translations, even early ones, in this chapter. I am guided both by chronology—the latest of the poems mentioned here is *Sospetto*—and by the fact that some poems, notably "Musicks Duell" and the hymns, are better discussed in other contexts.

24. Cf. Theodore Savory, *The Art of Translation* (Philadelphia: Dufour, 1960), pp. 39–40.

25. *Preface to Homer* (1610–1616), quoted in Cowl, p. 144.

26. "The Preface" to *Sylvae* (1685; rpt. Menston, Eng.: Scolar Press, 1973). Cf. Warren, *Richard Crashaw*, pp. 102–103.

27. Cf. Williams, *The Complete Poetry*, p. 199.

28. *Richard Crashaw*, pp. 132, 136–39.

29. Cf. Martin's discussion of the dating of *Sospetto*, pp. lxxxviii, xci.

30. See Mirollo, *The Poet of the Marvelous*, p. 74. Mirollo's book is an excellent introduction to *L'Adone* and *La Strage* in particular and to Marino in general and is a source of my remarks here.

31. On the date see Claes Schaar, *Marino and Crashaw, Sospetto d'Herode: A Commentary* (Lund: Gleerup, 1971), pp. 9–10.

32. Mirollo, p. 96. See his discussion of *La Strage*, pp. 95–97.

33. From the 1633 edition published in Venice.

34. In 1675 appeared a book titled *The Slaughter of the Innocents by Herod* . . . Newly Englished [by T.R.]. This version is a more literal rendering of the original and thus affords an interesting comparison not only to Marino but also to Crashaw.

35. Mirollo, pp. 159–60.

36. Warren thinks that Books III and IV "offer so much that was congenial to his temperament and his taste that Crashaw, one must suppose, began his translation with full intention of completing it" (*Richard Crashaw*, p. 120). Warren's judgment is, however, influenced by his belief that from Marino Crashaw realized his own "sacred muse."

37. Warren, *Richard Crashaw*, p. 121.

38. For certain details of the *Sospetto* I follow Claes Schaar's extensive notes in his edition and commentary.

39. Schaar suggests that Milton probably knew and used both versions of *Sospetto*. See his "The 'Sospetto d'Herode' and 'Paradise Lost,'" *English Studies* 50(1969): 511–16.

40. The studies of Warnke cited in Chapter 1 are particularly valuable in demonstrating the cross-fertilization of artistic styles between England and the Continent. In an unpublished dissertation, Robert V. Young argues for a greater recognition of the influence on Crashaw, particularly in his later verse, of the Spanish *Siglo de oro*, notably through the traditions of sacred parody and Gongorism. See "Richard Crashaw and the Spanish Golden Age," Diss. Yale Univ. 1972, p. 10 and *passim*.

41. Mirollo, p. 251. Two studies published in the 1950s questioned Marino's influence on English poetry in general and Crashaw in particular: Frank J. Warnke, "Marino and the English Metaphysicals," *Studies in the Renaissance* 2(1955): 160–75, and Laura Pettoello, "A Current Misconception Concerning the Influence of Marino's Poetry on Crashaw's," *Modern Language Review* 52(1957): 321–28. A recent note (Louis R. Barbato, "Marino, Crashaw, and *Sospetto d'Herode*," *Philological Quarterly* 54[1975]: 522–27) argues the older view that Crashaw was decisively influenced by Marino.

Chapter Three

1. *The Flaming Heart*, p. 238.

2. *Richard Crashaw*, p. 90.

3. Cf. Williams's discussion of the dating and circumstances of the two poems, *The Complete Poetry*, pp. 453–54.

4. My comments on the elegies are drawn from my article previously published as "Crashaw's Funeral Elegies" in Robert M. Cooper, ed., *Essays on Richard Crashaw*, Salzburg Studies in English Literature (Salzburg: Universität Salzburg, 1979), pp. 50–77.

5. The poem about which there is some doubt is the Latin "Epitaphium." Crashaw is the certain author but the subject may or may not be Herrys.

6. Crashaw's line has added impact when set against the traditional portrait of the Fates, the goddesses who controlled human destiny. Atropos cut the thread of life, an action that often carried with it a sense of whimsy or ruthlessness. Death's action in Crashaw's poem is notably peaceful and gentle.

7. Joseph H. Summers, *The Heirs of Donne and Jonson* (New York: Oxford Univ. Press, 1970), p. 109.

8. R. V. LeClerq's analysis of "Epithalamium" is a brilliant, although

sometimes too ingenious, study of the sacramental and numerological nature of the poem. See "Crashaw's 'Epithalamium,'" *Literary Monographs* 6(1975): 71–108.

9. Warren, *Richard Crashaw*, p. 110.

10. T. O. Beechcroft, "Crashaw and the Baroque Style," *Criterion* 13(1934): 415.

11. Warren, *Richard Crashaw*, pp. 108–109.

12. In "A Reading of 'Musicks Duell,'" in *Studies in Honor of John Wilcox*, ed. A. Dayle Wallace and Woodburn O. Ross (Detroit: Wayne State Univ. Press, 1958), pp. 39–50.

13. Summers, p. 107.

14. Martin, p. 183.

15. Although Morpheus, the god of dreams, is mentioned by name in the poem, his father, Somnus, was god of sleep. Crashaw might have intended either.

16. Cf. Praz, *The Flaming Heart*, p. 249.

Chapter Four

1. From Cowley's poem "On the Death of Mr. Crashaw."

2. Cf. Williams, *The Complete Poetry*, p. xxv.

3. Ibid., pp. 650–52.

4. Miner, p. 102.

5. Hamish Swanston has argued for a greater recognition of the similarities between Herbert and Crashaw in "The Second Temple," *Durham University Journal* 25(1963):14–22. His approach is rather unconvincing, as he attempts to show that Herbert is "Baroque."

6. Cf. Martin, p. 447, and Williams, *The Complete Poetry*, p. 86.

7. Although the texts are rhymed verse, I have followed Williams and his source in printing them as prose. See *The Complete Poetry*, pp. 96 and 666.

8. Ibid., p. 86.

9. Cf. Rosemond Tuve, *A Reading of George Herbert* (Chicago: Univ. of Chicago Press, 1952), p. 48.

10. *The Works of George Herbert*, ed. F. E. Hutchinson (Oxford, Eng.: The Clarendon Press, 1941).

11. From *The First Anniversary*, Frank Manley, ed., *John Donne: The Anniversaries* (Baltimore: The Johns Hopkins Press, 1963).

12. *European Metaphysical Poetry*, p. 23.

13. I have accepted the order of stanzas as published by Williams and, for ease of discussion, am assuming the alternating pattern of 1646 and 1648, although we cannot be sure, as Williams notes, that it is authorial in origin. For further discussion, see Clarence H. Miller, "The Order of Stanzas in Cowley and Crashaw's 'On Hope,'" *Studies in Philology*

61(1964): 64–73, and Williams, "The Order of Stanzas in Cowley and Crashaw's 'On Hope,'" *Studies in Bibliography* 22(1969): 207–10.

14. Miller, p. 69.
15. Ibid., p. 73.
16. "Some Influences in Crashaw's Poem 'On a Prayer Booke Sent to Mrs. M.R.,'" *Review of English Studies* 23(1947): 34–42. Allison, while noting the three influences of St. Teresa, the Song of Songs, and Carew, is also careful to assert that "Crashaw is as much indebted to the English seventeenth-century tradition as he is to St. Teresa"(36).
17. Allison, "Some Influences," p. 41.
18. Williams, *The Complete Poetry*, p. 146.
19. "Crashaw's Other Voice," *Studies in English Literature, 1500–1900* 9(1969): 136. Strier's article is excellent, one of the best analyses of a single Crashaw poem available.
20. The following comments derive from my discussion of "The Weeper" in "Crashaw's Two Weepers," *Concerning Poetry* 10:2(1977): 47–59.
21. *The Flaming Heart*, p. 218.
22. "Taste and Bad Taste in Metaphysical Poetry: Richard Crashaw and Dylan Thomas," in William R. Keast, ed., *Seventeenth-Century English Poetry: Modern Essays in Criticism* (New York: Oxford Univ. Press, 1962), pp. 264–79. Originally printed in *Hudson Review* 8(1955): 60–77.
23. *The Metaphysical Poets* (1936; rpt. New York: Collier Books, 1962), pp. 228–29.
24. Three critics who have posited varying readings and "defenses" of "The Weeper" are Stephen Manning, "The Meaning of 'The Weeper,'" *ELH* 22(1955): 34–47; Leland Chambers, "In Defense of 'The Weeper,'" *Papers on Language and Literature* 3(1967): 111–21; and Marc Bertonasco, "A New Look at Crashaw and 'The Weeper,'" *Texas Studies in Language and Literature* 10(1968): 177–88 (rpt. in his *Crashaw and the Baroque* (University, Ala.: Univ. of Alabama Press, 1971). Louis Martz has also reminded us of the "hyperbolical analogies" in other poems on the Magdalen's tears; it is at least necessary to be aware of the tradition before making quick condemnation (cf. *The Poetry of Meditation*, pp. 200–203).
25. Arno Esch's study of "The Weeper" in *Englische Religiöse Lyrik des 17. Jahrhunderts* (Tubingen: Max Niemeyer Verlag, 1955), is an important exception to the tendency to ignore the significance of the two versions. Esch argues that the second version is a notable improvement over the first (see pp. 105–17).
26. *The Flaming Heart*, p. 226.
27. The image has numerous antecedents. Cf. Martin, p. 433; Praz, *The Flaming Heart*, p. 220.
28. For comments on other changes see my article cited in n. 20.
29. "Poet and Saint," *TLS*, 1 June 1946, p. 258.

30. "Lope de Vega and *Las Lagrimas de la Madalena*," *Comparative Literature* 8(1956): 287ff.

31. Cf. Esch: "Mit dem Theme de Liebe hat Crashaw dem Gedicht ein neues Zentrum gegeben, das in der ersten Fassung uberhaupt keine Rolle spielte" (p. 111) (With the theme of love Crashaw has given the poem a new center, which in the first draft played no role at all).

Chapter Five

1. Quoted in Joseph Connelly, *Hymns of the Roman Liturgy* (Westminster, Md.: The Newman Press, 1957), pp. xiv-xv. Connelly also comments on the origins and development of the Latin hymns.

2. Puttenham, *The Arte of English Poesie*, pp. 21, 23.

3. Stanley Stewart's enlightening discussion of the poetic tradition emanating from the Song of Songs is found in his *The Enclosed Garden* (Madison: Univ. of Wisconsin Press, 1966), pp. 3–30.

4. See Praz, *The Flaming Heart*, p. 254. Eric Shepherd suggests the first explanation, Praz the second.

5. Cf. Sister Margaret Claydon, *Richard Crashaw's Paraphrases of Vexilla Regis, Stabat Mater, Adoro Te, Lauda Sion, Dies Irae, and O Gloriosa Domina*, Diss. Catholic Univ. of America 1960 (Washington, D.C.: Catholic Univ. of America Press, 1960), pp. 136–37. This study of the paraphrases is thorough and informative and deals with each poem in some detail. Also instructive are Esch's comments in *Englische Religiöse Lyrik*, pp. 142–59.

6. Cf. Warren, *Richard Crashaw*, p. 153. Also Praz, *The Flaming Heart*: "in place of the straightforward energy of the Latin text we find a winding circumlocution, which, though it has occasionally a cloying sweetness, and is clearly much less noble, does not lack a certain grace" (240).

7. In Cowl, p. 144.

8. See Connelly's discussion of the authorship, pp. 118–19.

9. The Latin originals are cited from Williams. I have also consulted the texts and translations in Connelly.

10. Claydon suggests that Thomas Car may be responsible for the stanzaic divisions; the poem appeared in 1648 without them (p. 33).

11. Claydon, pp. 75–76.

12. Cf. Warren, *Richard Crashaw*, p. 155; Williams, *The Complete Poetry*, p. 186.

13. Literally, "kneeling" and "bending low."

14. Connelly, p. 81.

15. Claydon, p. 130.

16. Connelly, p. 187.

17. Cf. Connelly, pp. 186–90, for a different version of the hymn.

18. Warren, *Richard Crashaw*, p. 156.

19. Ibid., pp. 156–58. Cf. Claydon, pp. 17–19.

20. Cf. Warren, *Richard Crashaw*, p. 157.

21. Cf. Connelly, p. 163.

22. The doctrine of the bodily Assumption of Mary is Roman, not Anglican, in origin, and it is the only example of non-Anglican dogma in Crashaw's verse. Whether he was a convert when he wrote the poem is, however, uncertain; some Anglicans, especially Laudians, accepted the doctrine of the Assumption, and Crashaw, given his affinity for the figure of the Virgin, would surely have found the doctrine appealing, even early on.

23. Cf. The Song of Songs 2:10–12.

24. See A. R. Cirillo, "Crashaw's 'Epiphany Hymn': The Dawn of Christian Time," *Studies in Philology* 67(1970): 67–88.

25. See *The Flaming Heart*, p. 255. Traditionally the *Jubilus* is assigned to St. Bernard, but see Connelly's dissenting discussion (and the text), pp. 58–65.

26. Martz, *The Poetry of Meditation*, pp. 352, 337–38.

27. In a slightly different vein, Cirillo discusses three distinct Incarnation experiences: the first coming of Christ *to* men, the coming of Christ *into* men through the Sacraments, and the final coming of Christ *against* men at Judgment Day (pp. 70–71).

28. Wallerstein, *Richard Crashaw*, p. 145.

29. Ibid., p. 146.

30. Kerby Neill, "Structure and Symbol in Crashaw's 'Hymn in the Nativity,'" *PMLA* 53(1948): 101–13, discusses the changes in the later version and argues that it shows "a growing sense of form" (101).

31. Cf. Williams's comments in *The Complete Poetry*, p. 37, and his *Image and Symbol in the Sacred Poetry of Richard Crashaw* (Columbia: Univ. of South Carolina Press, 1963), pp. 39, 52, 71.

32. Warren, *Richard Crashaw*, p. 151.

33. C. E. Rolt, trans. *Dionysius the Areopagite on the Divine Names and the Mystical Theology* (New York: Macmillan, 1920), pp. 191–92.

34. Warren, *Richard Crashaw*, p. 148.

Chapter Six

1. Quoted in Austin Warren, "Crashaw and St. Teresa," *TLS*, 25 August 1932, p. 593. Cf. Warren, *Richard Crashaw*, p. 44.

2. In addition to her *Vida*, a brief summary of her life is in Warren, *Richard Crashaw*, pp. 139–40, and a longer one in Petersson, *The Art of Ecstasy*, pp. 3–13.

3. Taken from the English translation of the *Vida* by "M. T." (presumably Tobie Matthew) (Antwerp: Hohannes Mersius, 1642), pp. 3–4.

Matthew first published his translation in 1623, a year after Teresa was
canonized and twelve years after the first English translation of the *Vida*
was published (also in Antwerp) in 1611. The title of Matthew's translation
(*The Flaming Hart or The Life of the Glorious S. Teresa*) likely gives the
title to the third of Crashaw's Teresa poems, and thus the poet would have
known the translation as well as the original. I have quoted from the copy
of *The Flaming Hart* in the Humanities Research Center at the University
of Texas at Austin.

4. Petersson, p. 3.
5. Ibid.
6. Ibid., p. 14.
7. Ibid., p. 4.
8. Preface to *The Flaming Hart*, par. 22.
9. *The Flaming Hart*, p. 107.
10. Ibid., p. 108.
11. Ibid.
12. Ibid., pp. 248–49.
13. Petersson, p. 12 and p. 167, n. 12.
14. *The Flaming Hart*, pp. 419–21.
15. Cf. Petersson, pp. 9ff.
16. Ibid., p. 11.
17. Quoted in Petersson, p. 7.
18. The phrase is cited in Petersson, p. 4, without attribution.
19. In the 1648 *Steps* "The Flaming Heart" follows the Hymn (that in
1646 and 1648 has the title "In memory of the vertuous and Learned Lady
Madre de Teresa that sought an early Martyrdome"), and the "Apologie"
is thus made for both "precedent Hymns." The 1652 placement of the
"Apologie" between the two major poems is aesthetically more satisfying.
20. See Warren, *Richard Crashaw*, p. 140.
21. Petersson calls the Hymn Crashaw's "most accomplished, most
fully developed work" (127); Warren sees it as "one of Crashaw's four or
five best pieces" (*Richard Crashaw*, p. 146); and Martz judges it "one of
Crashaw's perfect poems" (*The Wit of Love*, p. 135).
22. A portion of the following comments was delivered as a paper to the
South-Central Renaissance Conference in March 1978.
23. *Waiting on God*, trans. Emma Craufurd (London: Routledge &
Kegan Paul, 1951), p. 108. Cf. Petersson, p. 135.
24. My interest in Teresa's sexual identity is an attempt to place her
poetic roles in view of conventional seventeenth-century notions about the
"feminine" and the "masculine." Thus for these purposes I adopt (as did
Crashaw) the conventional associations of the feminine with the passive,
the soft, the weak; the masculine with the active, the forceful, the strong. I
do not promote the accuracy of those associations.
25. Cf. Petersson, p. 130, for slightly different line divisions.

26. Ibid., p. 134.

27. Cf. Robert Collmer's discussion of "Crashaw's 'Death More Mystical and High,'" *JEGP* 55(1956): 373–80.

28. *The Flaming Hart*, pp. 420–21.

29. Cf. Warren, *Richard Crashaw*, p. 144.

30. *The Flaming Heart*, p. 261.

31. Martz states the achievement even more strongly: "The earlier poem on Saint Teresa achieves its success by a subtle blending of the art of Ben Jonson with the mystical fervor of Saint Teresa, but this kind of easy blending is almost unique in Crashaw's work" (*The Wit of Love*, p. 135).

32. Cf. Williams, *Image and Symbol*, pp. 92–93, and Allison, "Crashaw and St. François de Sales," pp. 295–300.

33. From *Conceptions of the Love of God*, in *The Complete Works of Saint Teresa of Jesus*, trans. and ed. E. Allison Peers (London: Sheed & Ward, 1946), II, 391.

34. Cf. Rosemond Tuve, *A Reading of George Herbert*, pp. 112ff.

35. From *Le Traité de L'Amour de Dieu*, Book I, Chapter 6. Cited in Allison, "Crashaw and St. François de Sales," pp. 299–300. For a broader view of Salesian influence on Crashaw, see Marc Bertonasco, *Crashaw and the Baroque*, pp. 55–82.

36. Wallerstein, *Richard Crashaw*, p. 10.

37. Praz, *The Flaming Heart*, p. 262.

38. Louis Martz has proposed (in *The Wit of Love*) a particular painting (Gerhard Seghers's *St. Teresa in Ecstasy*) as the object of Crashaw's attention. The painting no doubt fits the poem, as do others.

Epilogue

1. Warren, *Richard Crashaw*, p. 142. For the Litany I quote from John E. Booty, ed., *The Book of Common Prayer (1559)* (Charlottesville: Univ. Press of Virginia, 1976), p. 69.

Selected Bibliography

PRIMARY SOURCES

1. Principal Seventeenth-Century Editions

Epigrammatum Sacrorum Liber. Cambridge, 1634.

Steps to the Temple. Sacred Poems, With other Delights of the Muses. London, 1646.

Steps to the Temple. . . . The second Edition wherein are added divers pieces not before extant. London, 1648.

Carmen Deo Nostro. Paris, 1652.

A Letter from Mr. Crashaw to the Countess of Denbigh, Against Irresolution and Delay in matters of Religion. London, 1653(?).

Richardi Crashawi Poemata et Epigrammata. . . . Editio Secunda, Auctior & emendatior. Cambridge, 1670. A second edition of the Greek and Latin epigrams.

Steps to the Temple, The Delights Of The Muses, and Carmen Deo Nostro. . . . The 2^d Edition. London, 1670. An erroneously titled "second" edition of the poems.

2. Principal Modern Editions

The Complete Works of Richard Crashaw, ed. Alexander B. Grosart. 2 vols. Fuller Worthies Library. London: Printed for Private Circulation, 1872–73. A historically important edition, useful for its discussion of early texts and Crashaw's life.

Steps to the Temple, Delights of the Muses, and other Poems, ed. A. R. Waller. Cambridge: Cambridge Univ. Press, 1904. Of some historical interest, but marked by carelessness.

The Poems English, Latin, and Greek of Richard Crashaw, ed. L. C. Martin. 2d ed. Oxford: The Clarendon Press, 1957. An authoritative and reliable edition.

The Complete Poetry of Richard Crashaw, ed. George Walton Williams. 1970; rpt. New York: Norton, 1974. Originally published in the Anchor Seventeenth-Century Series. Competes with Martin as the standard edition. Includes generic and topical arrangements, and both sources and translations.

SECONDARY SOURCES

1. Books
BERTONASCO, MARC F. *Crashaw and the Baroque*. University, Ala.: Univ. of Alabama Press, 1971. An examination of Crashaw's poetry in light of the Baroque, the emblem tradition, and Salesian meditation.
CLAYDON, SISTER MARGARET. *Richard Crashaw's Paraphrases of Vexilla Regis, Stabat Mater, Adoro Te, Lauda Sion, Dies Irae, and O Gloriosa Domina*. Diss. Catholic Univ. of America 1960. Washington, D.C.: Catholic Univ. of America Press, 1960. A thorough and insightful analysis of Crashaw's paraphrases of the six medieval Latin hymns.
ELLRODT, ROBERT. *John Donne et Les Poètes de la Tradition Chrétienne*. Paris: Librairie José Corti, 1960. Book I of a significant two-volume study, *Les Poètes Métaphysiques Anglais*. Focuses on Donne but discusses Crashaw.
ESCH, ARNO. *Englische Religiöse Lyrik des 17. Jahrhunderts*. Tubingen: Max Niemeyer Verlag, 1955. A comprehensive and valuable study containing chapters on Crashaw's sacred poems, notably the paraphrases of medieval hymns.
MARTZ, LOUIS L. *The Poetry of Meditation*. 2d ed. New Haven: Yale Univ. Press, 1962. The definitive study of the "meditative tradition," with an important analysis of the Hymn to the Name of Jesus.
——. *The Wit of Love*. Notre Dame: The Univ. of Notre Dame Press, 1969. Lectures on Donne, Marvell, Carew, and Crashaw, and a chapter on the Baroque quality of the Hymn to St. Teresa.
MILHAUPT, SISTER MARIS STELLA. "The Latin Epigrams of Richard Crashaw." Diss. University of Michigan, 1963. A review of the history of the sacred epigram, with a discussion of the order of Crashaw's poems. Includes translations.
PETERSSON, ROBERT T. *The Art of Ecstasy*. 1970; rpt. New York: Atheneum, 1974. An illuminating interpretation of St. Teresa, Bernini, and Crashaw, focusing on the cross-fertilization of art forms.
PRAZ, MARIO. *The Flaming Heart*. 1958; rpt. New York: Norton, 1973. An important book on the relations between Italian and English literature. Includes Praz's influential essay on Crashaw and the Baroque.
RICKEY, MARY ELLEN. *Rhyme and Meaning in Richard Crashaw*. Lexington: Univ. of Kentucky Press, 1961. A useful study of rhyming patterns in Crashaw's verse.
SCHAAR, CLAES. *Marino and Crashaw, Sospetto d'Herode: A Commentary*. Lund: G. W. K. Gleerup, 1971. A comparison of Marino's original and Crashaw's translation, with extensive notes and commentary.
WALLERSTEIN, RUTH. *Richard Crashaw: A Study in Style and Poetic Development*. Univ. of Wisconsin Studies in Lang. and Lit., No. 37. Madison: Univ. of Wisconsin Press, 1935. One of the earliest, and best, studies of the increasing maturity of Crashaw's verse.

WARREN, AUSTIN. *Richard Crashaw: A Study in Baroque Sensibility.* University, La: Louisiana State Univ. Press, 1939. The definitive study of Crashaw and the Baroque.

WILLIAMS, GEORGE WALTON. *Image and Symbol in the Sacred Poetry of Richard Crashaw.* Columbia: Univ. of South Carolina Press, 1963. A somewhat mechanical, but useful, study of the types and frequency of imagery in Crashaw's poetry.

2. Articles Generally on Crashaw

ADAMS, ROBERT M. "Taste and Bad Taste in Metaphysical Poetry: Richard Crashaw and Dylan Thomas," *Hudson Review* 8 (1955): 60–77. Rpt. in William Keast, ed. *Seventeenth-Century English Poetry: Modern Essays in Criticism.* New York: Oxford Univ. Press, 1962, pp. 264–79. An indictment of the occasions of "bad taste" in Crashaw's verse, notably in the epigram on Luke 11 and "The Weeper."

ALLISON, ANTHONY F. "Crashaw and St. François de Sales," *Review of English Studies* 24(1948): 295–302. A convincing argument for the influence of St. François de Sales on some of Crashaw's later works.

LARSEN, KENNETH J. "Richard Crashaw's *Epigrammata Sacra*," in J. W. Binns, ed. *The Latin Poetry of English Poets.* London: Routledge & Kegan Paul, 1974, pp. 93–120. An interpretive study of the increasingly Laudian theology implicit in the chronology of the epigrams.

McCANLES, MICHAEL. "The Rhetoric of the Sublime in Crashaw's Poetry," in Thomas O. Sloan and Raymond B. Waddington, eds. *The Rhetoric of Renaissance Poetry.* Berkeley: Univ. of California Press, 1974, pp. 189–211. A sensitive analysis of rhetorical effects, especially hyperbole, in Crashaw. Through hyperbole Crashaw views both eros and agape.

PETTOELLO, LAURA. "A Current Misconception Concerning the Influence of Marino's Poetry on Crashaw's," *Modern Language Review* 52(1957): 321–28. One of several studies of the last several decades that seek to diminish the effects of Marino's poetry on Crashaw's.

RASPA, ANTHONY. "Crashaw and the Jesuit Poetic," *University of Toronto Quarterly* 36(1966): 37–54. Aligns Crashaw's poetry and the "Jesuit poetic tradition" through the "epigrammatic style."

3. Articles on Individual Poems

ALLISON, ANTHONY F. "Some Influences in Crashaw's Poem 'On a Prayer-Booke sent to Mrs. M. R.,'" *Review of English Studies* 23(1947): 34–42. A study of the various influences on Crashaw's poem, including St. Teresa, the Song of Songs, and Carew's "A Rapture."

CHAMBERS, LELAND. "In Defense of 'The Weeper,'" *Papers on Language and Literature* 3(1967): 111–21. Stresses the importance of the emblem tradition for the poem, particularly the emblem of the Sacred Heart of God.

CIRILLO, A. R. "Crashaw's 'Epiphany Hymn': The Dawn of Christian Time," *Studies in Philology* 67(1970): 67-88. A penetrating view of the Epiphany Hymn as "the liturgical climax of the incarnation cycle— the celebration of the inner manifestation of the second advent."

COLLMER, ROBERT G. "Crashaw's 'Death More Mysticall and High,'" *Journal of English and Germanic Philology* 55(1956): 373-80. Death in the Hymn to St. Teresa seen as mystical union with God.

FARNHAM, ANTHONY E. "Saint Teresa and the Coy Mistress," *Boston University Studies in English* 2(1956): 226-39. A comparative study of the Marvell and Crashaw poems, drawing from them a "conceptual distinction of classical and Christian."

JAUERNICK, STEFANIE. "Crashaw's Hymne auf Santa Teresa," *Die Neueren Sprachen* 14(1965): 449-61. An analysis of the Hymn and its association with the life ("Lebens") and teaching ("Lehre") of the saint.

LECLERQ, R. V. "Crashaw's 'Epithalamium': Pattern and Vision," *Literary Monographs* 6(1975): 71-108. An insightful, although sometimes overly ingenious, study of the poem, with much attention to numerological patterns.

MADSEN, WILLIAM G. "A Reading of 'Musicks Duell,'" in A. Dayle Wallace and Woodburn O. Ross, eds. *Studies in Honor of John Wilcox.* Detroit: Wayne State Univ. Press, 1958, pp. 39-50. Contrasts the music of the nightingale and the man on several levels, most importantly with a theological emphasis.

MANNING, STEPHEN. "The Meaning of 'The Weeper,'" *ELH* 22(1955): 34-47. Focuses on the theme of "spiritual perfection" in the poem, the mystical progress of the soul toward union with the deity.

NEILL, KERBY. "Structure and Symbol in Crashaw's 'Hymn in the Nativity,'" *PMLA* 63(1948): 101-13. Emphasizes the superiority of the second version of the Nativity Hymn; it is more theological and symbolic in its portraits.

PARRISH, PAUL A. "Crashaw's Two Weepers," *Concerning Poetry* 10: 2(1977): 47-59. An analysis of the two versions of "The Weeper," showing that the final version has greater cohesion and direction.

PETER, JOHN. "Crashaw and 'The Weeper,'" *Scrutiny* 19(1953): 258-73. Comments on the problem of "mere ingenuity" in Crashaw's imagery.

SCHWENGER, PETER. "Crashaw's Perspectivist Metaphor," *Comparative Literature* 28(1976): 65-74. A study of metaphors, notably in "The Weeper," that have a cumulative effect, "each image unfolding out of its predecessor."

STRIER, RICHARD. "Crashaw's Other Voice," *Studies in English Literature, 1500-1900* 9(1969): 135-51. An excellent analysis of the 1652 poem to the Countess of Denbigh as an example of Crashaw's "other voice," revealing evidence of tension and introspection.

Index